3D Modeling

Blender Basics by Example

Justin John Hay

Manufactured in the United States of America

CONTENTS

Blender is a robust 3D modeling program, which is both free and open source. Three dimensional meshes, animations, and even video games are possible with Blender. Regarding the latter, people are often surprised to hear of Blender's built in game engine, not to mention the Python (scripting language) editor. Blender is a fully packed, feature rich 3d suite. Considering Blender's free status, it is a stunning example of what can be accomplished with open source software.

With the Blender builds becoming increasingly feature packed, problems with teaching, and more importantly, problems with learning are becoming evident. A beginners book on Blender 3D modeling could easily occupy 3-4 volumes, each containing 900 pages. This is what so often occurs in other scientific fields, such as computer programming, -whereby 2,500 page books are dumped onto beginners. Inevitably, the beginners burn out by the end, oftentimes forgetting what they learned in the early going. The result is often failure. **It is a matter of too much volume!** This work serves to bypass the problem at hand. Only the very core modeling techniques are shown; all else is forsaken. Topics such as advanced texturing, the new Cycles rendering engine, nodes, and the like, are purposefully sidestepped. This is done in an effort to avoid the burnout and get modelers off the ground within a few weeks.

The teaching style relies on small technique based examples, for which readers are to work through and replicate. Full models are not used to demonstrate technique, -this alone speeds the learning process considerably. However, it is extremely valuable to go through and replicate a few models. At the end of the book, 5 small, but complete models are given with step-by-step instruction. While following step-by-step instructions is tedious, it allows for a small period, whereby modelers are essentially using training-wheels. This saves the agony of transferring from 'technique understanding' to 'full on' model development. Given models were chosen for their relative simplicity, and moderately low vertex counts. Regarding the latter, consideration was given to those on less powerful machines.

INSTALLATION INSTRUCTIONS **Must Read**

Blender software releases do not work in the same manner as other types of software. The Blender Foundation is constantly churning out new releases. Thus, new releases are not as important with Blender as they are with other types other software. This book is based on **Blender 2.62 and should only be used with 2.62.** Up to version 2.62, Blender is using the older core modeling system using only triangles and quads. After 2.62, Blender has integrated the new core modeling system called B-Mesh, which supports n-gons. The old system should be learned first, which will make the new B-Mesh system easy to understand. Do not attempt to use newer versions (with B-Mesh) with this book. B-Mesh will be addressed in the last chapter of this book.

Download Blender 2.62 at http://download.blender.org/release/Blender2.62/

Note: Manually navigating to the above link can be achieve by going to www.blender.org -then clicking **Download → Older Versions.**

Windows Users will download either:
blender-2.62-release-windows32.exe **(for 32 bit systems)**
blender-2.62-release-windows64.exe **(for modern 64 bit systems)**
** **Determining system type can be done by going to Start → Control Panel → System and Maintenance → System**

Mac Users will download either:
blender-2.62-release-OSX_10.5_i386.zip
Mac Pro, MacBook, MacBook Pro, iMac(Intel)

blender-2.62-release-OSX_10.5_ppc.zip
(PowerMac G5, Powerbook G4, iMac G5) Requires OS X 10.5+

blender-2.62-release-OSX_10.6_x86_64.zip **(for modern 64 bit systems)**
(Intel Core 2 Duo, Intel Quad-Core/Duel-Core Xeon, Core i3/i5, i7) Requires OS X 10.6+

Mac User Input Instructions
Main Windows key command substitutions for Mac
- **Command key** replaces the **Control key** in widows.
- Rendering is done via the F12 key. Some Machines use this key to eject the DVD player. For those with this issue, use Ctrl + F12 or Alt + F12 for rendering.

Mac Mice
Standard 3 button mice are recommended for use with Blender. Using Mac single button mice, or the Magic Mouse, while possible via emulation, and/or with 3rd party applications should be avoided.

Laptops Without Numpads
Blender does not treat the numbers above the home-row as having the same functionality as the numbers on the numpad. For those using keyboards without numpads, the following setting is required. Go to File → User Preferences → Input → and put a check beside Emulate Numpad.
Note: This setting functionally changes the numbers above the home-row into a numpad.

Warning: Mandatory Setting Change for Blender!
In recent versions of Blender, the regular method of rotating meshes, otherwise known as Orbit Style, has been set to Turntable. This default setting is non-intuitive for the manipulation of mesh objects. Once Blender is installed, please change it to Trackball; In the top left, go to File → User Preferences → Input → and under Orbit Style, click on Trackball, and then click the "Save as Default" button.

Chapter 1: Blender's GUI

Once installed, fire up Blender. What you will see is a default cube in perspective view.

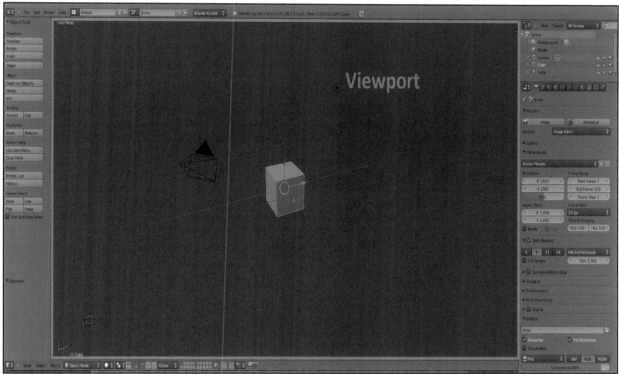

The frame in which the cube sits (shown with a red rectangle) is called the viewport. This is where all the modeling takes place. What is important for any beginner to know, is that the cursor must be inside the viewport when making changes (e.g., selecting, scaling, or rotating an object). Think of this as placing it in an "accept command" state. Computer programmers refer to this as focus. By default, Blender starts out with a cube, camera, lamp, and a grid floor.

3D Modeling

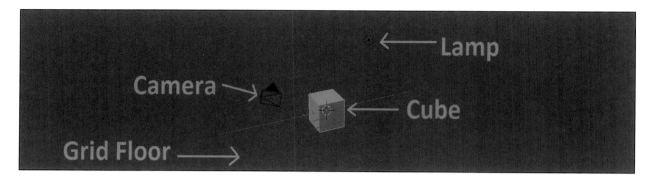

The objects can be selected by right clicking on them. Go ahead and do so for the camera, lamp, and back again to the cube. Notice how selected objects always turn to orange. Only selected objects **may** have actions and modifications done to them. Unselected objects are ignored.

That 3-arrow thingy situated inside the cube is called a translate manipulator.

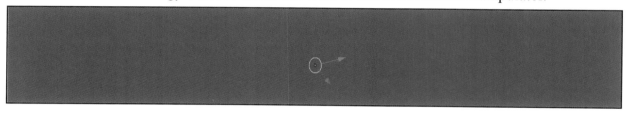

It functions as a mesh's axial compass to aid movement, scaling, and extrusion along any given axis (X, Y, Z). Experience has taught that it is better not to use this during the beginning stages. It tends to obscure the view, and helps very little. Axial orientation tends to be confusing for beginners, -no matter what. That being said, get rid of it. Hit Control + Space bar, and poof, it is gone.

Oh my, it would seem there was something left over in the cube. This little red n' white circle with cross-hairs is called the 3D Cursor.

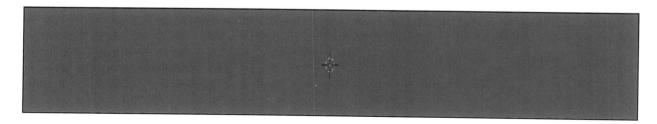

It is different from the mouse cursor, so don't get the two confused. The 3D cursor can be thought of a placeholder for pivoting and scaling. Additionally, whenever a new object is created, it is placed at the position of the 3d cursor. This cursor can be moved. Left click anywhere in the 3D viewport and move it.

To the left of the viewport is the tool shelf. This serves as a quick access panel for different modeling tools.

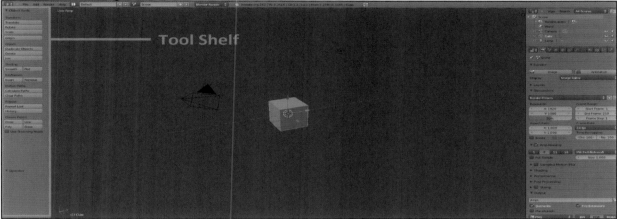

The tool shelf is a little tricky in that it changes options when moving from Object Mode to Edit Mode. The Tool shelf pane can be hidden by hitting the T key. Hit the T Key again, and it will reappear. It can also be minimized by grabbing the pane edge (hold left mouse button and dragging to the left.

The next area a concern is the buttons panel. This is the nerve center of Blender, where all the magic happens. There are a lot of buttons there, but for beginners, nothing more than a few need consideration.

Render Button: This is the 1st button, -with the camera icon. This panel provides options when rendering 3D images. A plethora are available by default, and this panel can be avoided entirely by hitting the render shortcut, the F12 key. However, there is one setting which beginners may want to change; that is the render resolution percentage. It is currently (they seem to change it with each release) set to 50%. Generally speaking, image quality should always be at 100%. At least for the final render.

World Button: The World button (globe icon) will mainly be used to set the background color for rendered images. There are also extra settings for advanced lighting, along with a few other bells n' whistles.

Modifier Button: Signified by the wrench icon, this panel will allow modifiers to be used. Modifiers are automated tools for making changes to the mesh. Examples of this are beveling, and curves. One modifier in particular will be used a great deal. It is called the Subdivision Surface Modifier. It automatically smooths objects by increasing the geometric complexity. It is a great tool, albeit a computationally expensive one!

Material Button: Signified by a nondescript golden icon, this panel will mainly be used for adding mesh colors, along with controlling light reflection.

Textures Button: One to the right of the material button, the texture panel (red checker board icon) is, as it name implies, for adding textures. Want to add a cloth texture to a pillow case, -this is where it is done. Some textures (not all) come with an extra information called **normals.** The **normal values** can raise up or indent a parts of the texture. This adds a whole lot of realism by decreasing the flat look.

There are also a few other items of immediate importance for beginners to become acquainted with.

Add: This is where new meshes and lamps are added to the scene. Blender has simple built in shapes such as cubes, circles, cones, and tubes to begin modeling with. Blender even has a pre-modeled face of a monkey named Suzanne. Suzanne oftentimes comes in handy as a test mesh for all kinds of things. It is not always practical to build an entire mesh just to test out a color, texture, or lighting scene. This "ADD" menu also has text, curves, armature bones, and a whole lot more. Throughout the exercises in this book, constant references will be made to delete the default cube and add "whatever shape to start out with."

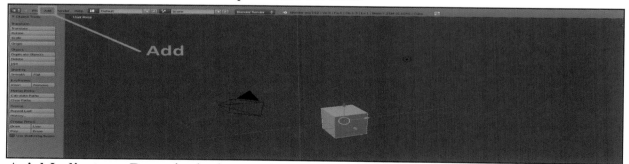

Axial Indicator: Down in the bottom left is the axial indicator. A weather vane of sorts for showing axial direction. Users can look down at it while modeling to tell where the X, Y, and Z axis is currently located. It serves the same function as the translate manipulator, but does not get in the way. That being said, the axial indicator is all that is needed for finding X, Y, and Z orientations. Place the mouse cursor in the viewport, hold down the middle mouse button and move the mouse around. The axial orientation is locked to the mesh.

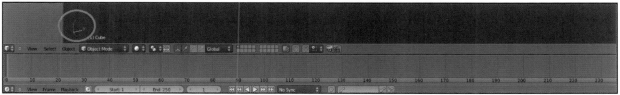

Mode: As is sensible, Mode displays the current mode. Beginners will mainly be using the two main modes, which are Object and Edit Mode. Object Mode is what Blender starts out in by default, and may be thought of as a general starting point for object creation and object selection, while Edit Mode is where all the mesh manipulation takes place. This is a difficult concept for beginners to grasp, as need for this mode separation is not completely intuitive.

Here are some key points to remember about MODE.

1: Hitting Tab switches between Object Mode and Edit Mode.
2: When adding additional meshes to a scene, Object Mode is generally utilized. When adding additional meshes in Edit Mode, Blender will consider it to be linked to the original mesh. Scale one, and the other will be scaled. Grab one, and the other will move with it (as though they are linked in thin air). Again, this is usually unwanted, and avoided by adding new meshes in Object Mode. Once added, each mesh must be selected, then tab into into Edit Mode to begin modeling. In other words, only one mesh can be modeled at a time. If you want to model the other mesh, you must go back into Object Mode, select it, and then go back into Edit Mode. It all sounds cumbersome, but the process is quick with a little practice.
3: Certain objects, such as lamps and cameras, can only be selected in Object Mode.
4: Watch out for the "gotcha problem" that newcomers face. At some point during modeling, you will accidentally select a camera or lamp (generally to move them) and forget to select the object you were modeling. When trying to get back into Edit Mode to do some addition modeling, the mesh won't accept commands. **The object to be modeled must be selected, not the camera or lamp**. Remember this one, because there is a 100% chance that it is going to happen.

3D Modeling

Vertex, Edge, Face Select: When selecting part(s) of a mesh, there is more than one choice on how to do it. The actual intersection points can be selected, the edges, or the entire panel which makes up the face. These buttons are pretty self explanatory. Your job is to remember their location, nothing more.

Limit Selection to Visible: This setting allows or disallows visibility of the mesh's background geometry. It is only available in Edit Mode. The **Off** state allows for the mesh to be seen all the way through. It also allows all the vertices in the back of the mesh to be selected. The **On** state only allows the vertices in front to be seen and selected. The Limit Selection to Visible button functions as a toggle switch.

Limit Selection to Visible **On**

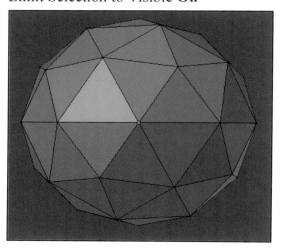

Limit Selection to Visible **Off**

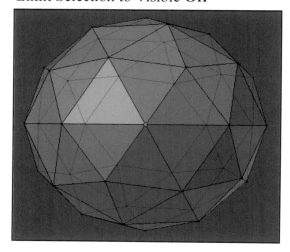

Blender's GUI

Border selecting when **On** (tilted view)

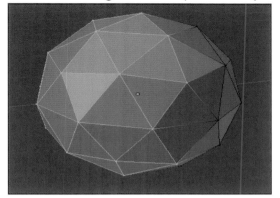

Border selecting when **Off**

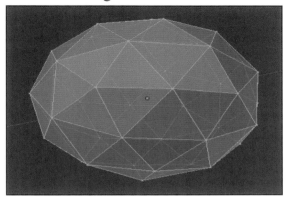

Chapter 2: Controlling the View

Exercise # 1 Perspective vs. Orthographic View

When Blender starts, it is always in Perspective View. Perspective View is how all of us see in real life, -with objects in the distance being smaller, and those in the foreground, larger. Blender designers purposely start out this way to stress the 3d nature of the program. However valuable for newcomers, it's an annoyance for the rest of us. Most modeling will be done in Orthographic View. The differences are demonstrated here:

Step 1: Start a new Blender scene (File → New), and tab into Edit Mode, and hit 1 on the numpad.
Step 2: Make sure Limit Selection to Visible is **Off**.
Step 3: Hit 5 on the Numpad and switch into Orthographic View. Everything should be aligned to the grid, and this is how you will want to start out.
Note: Throughout the first few chapters, you will always be instructed to hit the 5 key on the numpad to get out of Perspective View.

Exercise # 2 Manually Changing the View

When view is spoken of, more is being assumed than just Perspective or Orthographic presentations. View also relates to top, front, bottom, right, left, and back. These are the normal expected viewing angles. Let's manually change the view of the cube.
Step 1: Place the mouse pointer anywhere near the cube, but not on it, and hold down the

middle mouse button (MMB). Drag the mouse in any direction. The cube should spin. Easy enough.

Exercise # 3 Automatic View Changing with the Numpad

Changing the view by holding down the Middle Mouse Button and dragging the mouse works well, but sometimes proper alignment is needed. Changing between top, front, and right can be done on the Numpad.

Step 1: Start a new scene (file → New) and tab into Edit Mode, hit 5 (numpad) to get out of perspective mode.

Step 2: Practice switching views by hitting 7, 1, and 3 on the numpad. This must be done on the numpad and not on the number row above the keyboard (they have different functions).

Step 3: Now experiment with 2 and 8 on the number pad. They incrementally move the view upward and downward. Then 4 and 6 on the numpad to increment left or right.

Exercise # 4 Zooming-In and Zooming-Out

Step 1: With the mouse cursor in the 3d viewport, simply scroll the the middle mouse button forward or backward. Do not hold the middle mouse button down when doing so.

Exercise # 5 Panning

Learn this, memorize it and love it, for it will be needed. Sometimes in Blender, an object can be too far off to the right, left, or up/down. To remedy this, the view can be panned up, down, left or right.

Step 1: Make sure the cube is selected (glowing), if not, hit the "A" key.

Step 2: Place the mouse cursor anywhere near or on the cube.

Step 3: Hold down the shift key, then hold down the Middle Mouse Button. With both being held, move the mouse around.

Step 4: Just for fun, let go of the of the shift button and zoom in and out (scroll Middle Mouse Button). These two procedures will oftentimes be used in conjunction.

Exercise # 6 Camera Viewing

Step 1: Start a new scene, File → New, and hit the Zero key on the numpad, this is the view which will be rendered. You are looking through the camera right now.

Step 2: Hit the "G" key and grab the cube. Very cool, the cube can be moved (via the mouse) even when looking through the camera. Left click to finalize the grab function.

Step 3: Right click on the outer box frame of the camera. The black line should start glowing and the box should now be unselected.

Step 4: Hit the "G" key again, and move the camera around. Pretty slick.

Step 5: Hit F12 to render the scene and then hit Escape to exit.

Step 6: Time to get out of camera mode. Hit the 7 key and the viewport will return to the top view. Hit tab and try to switch to Edit Mode. Nothing happens! It won't switch to Edit Mode because the camera is selected, and when this occurs, Edit Mode will not be available.

Step 7: Right mouse click on the box, and it should now glow. Now hit tab, and go into Edit Mode. Pay attention to this. As stated before, this is a very common mistake for beginners when in Object Mode.

Pro Tip: Positioning the camera is generally not done while looking through it, as that is a fine adjustment. The camera can be set to view exactly what you are viewing at any given time. This is a very handy little feature. To do so, hit CNTRL + ALT + 0.

Chapter 3: Basic Mesh Operations

Learning to modify meshes is perhaps the most rewarding experience for newcomers. After getting a sense of how general shapes can be made, scaled, spun, and smoothed, -beginners start to really get of sense of what 3d modeling is all about. These basics are the underpinning for everything in 3d modeling. Learn them well. Before beginning, make a conscious note of one thing, -this is where the modeling begins and where the mistakes start happening. **CNTRL + Z** (Undo Feature) is you dearest friend at this point.

Exercise # 1 Entire Mesh Selecting and Deselecting
Step 1: Start a new scene, File → New. Hit 5, then 1 on the numpad. Hit Tab to go into Edit Mode.
Step 2: Hit the "A" key and switch between "selected" and "unselected." Notice how the cube no longer glows orange when unselected. When selected, the **entire** cube accepts commands.

Exercise # 2 Grabbing/Moving Objects
Step 1: Start a new scene, File → New. Hit 5, then 1 on the numpad. Hit Tab to go into Edit Mode.
Step 2: The cube should be selected and glowing orange, if not, hit the A key. Place the mouse cursor anywhere on or near the cube and hit the "G" key. Move the mouse and the cube should follow.
Step 3: Click the Left Mouse Button to drop the cube in any desired location. Moving meshes is extremely simple.

Exercise # 3 Rotating Objects

Step 1: Start a new scene, File → New. Hit 5, then 1 on the numpad. Hit Tab to go into Edit Mode.

Step 2: They cube should already be selected, if not, hit the A key.

Step 3: Place the mouse cursor in the viewport and hit the "R" key. Move the mouse to rotate.

Step 4: Hit R again, then the "X" key, and now move the mouse. The rotation is now constrained to the "X" axis. Left click to finalize the rotation.

Step 5: Hit R again, then the "Y" key, and now move the mouse. The rotation is now constrained to the "Y" axis. Left click to finalize the rotation.

Step 6: Hit R again, then then the "Z" key, and now move the mouse. The rotation is now constrained to the "Z" axis. Left click to finalize the rotation.

Note: Getting comfortable with rotating objects comes with practice. It is important to understand the difference between rotating objects vs changing the view (via holding the middle mouse button (with mouse movement)) or numpad selection. When rotating objects, the object moves independently of the view. Notice how the grid does not move when rotating objects, but does so when changing the view.

Exercise # 4 Manual Selection of Vertices (with Extrusion)

Step 1: Start a new scene, File → New, then hit tab to go into Edit Mode.

Step 2: Hit 5 on the numpad, then 1 on the numpad.

Step 3: Tap the "A" key once to deselect all vertices.

Step 4: Holding the Middle Mouse Button, tip the view to show the top of the cube.

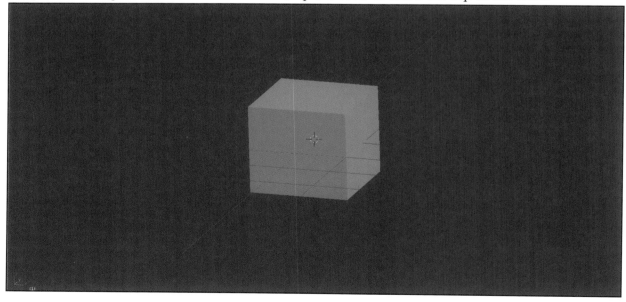

Basic Mesh Operations

Step 5: Now, Right Mouse Click one of the top corners. If done correctly, the lines extending from the vertex should have turned orange. The vertex is now selected. See pic.

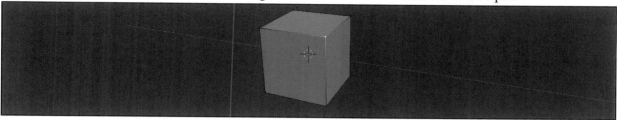

Step 6: To select the other three vertices on the top, hold down the SHFT key and Right Mouse Click each of them once. The entire top surface of the cube should now be selected and glowing. If not, go back through the steps.

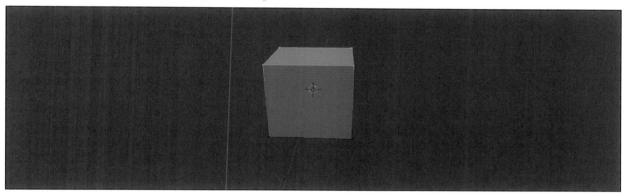

Step 7: With the top face of square glowing (all vertices selected), hit the 1 key (on numpad) to get back into front view. Hit the "E" key to extrude. Push the mouse forward and size the new cube the same as the first. Left click when the size is correct. Two blocks should be stacked on top of each other. Keep it neat.

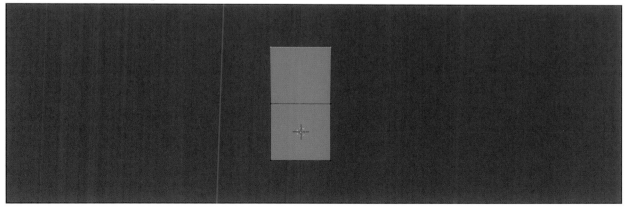

3D Modeling

Step 8: Repeat the same procedure three more times. Make sure the top four vertices are selected, hit the "E" key and extrude up another block. Keep going until five are stacked on top of each other. A tilted view is shown.

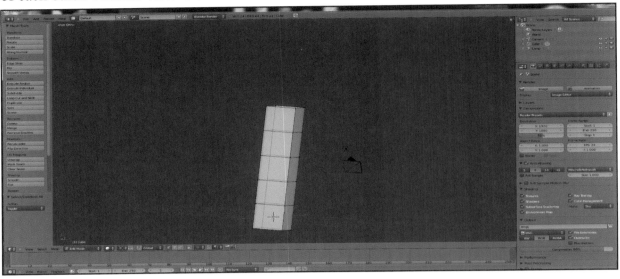

Step 9: From here, the letter "T" will be formed. Tap the A key to deselect the top vertices and Tilt the scene with the Middle Mouse Button as in the photo below. Select the 4 vertices on the side of the top block by holding SHFT and Right clicking.

Step 10: With all 4 vertices selected, hit 1 on the numpad. Hit E and extrude out 2 more cubes of the same size.

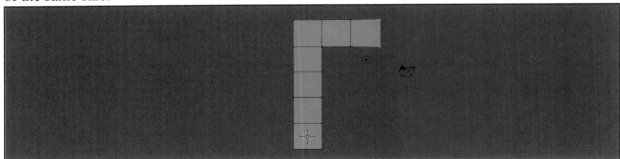

Basic Mesh Operations

Optionally, one single large extrusion could have been done, but 2 is fine. Tap A when done.

Step 11: Do the same for the opposite side, and form the left hand side of the letter T. When done, this should be the basic shape.

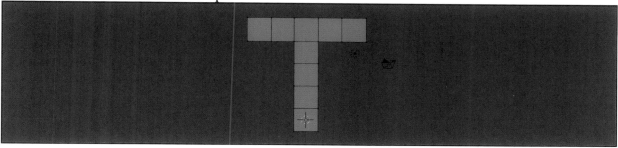

Step 12: It's time to set up the scene for rendering, hit 0 on the numpad to check the camera view. It is way off from what will give a good image render. That is fine, hit 1 on the numpad, then TAB into Object Mode. Zoom out by scrolling the middle mouse button. Right click on the camera, and hit the G key. Move it up and to the right, -that should give a better view.

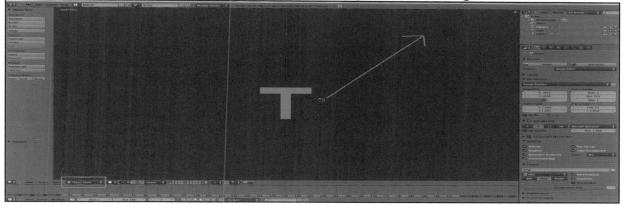

Step 13: Hit zero again on the numpad and make sure the "T" is visible. Again, when viewing from the camera, the outer viewing square can be clicked on, and then moved via the G key. When the "T" is well centered, Hit F12 and render the image.

Step 14: Why is the "T" so dark? The lamp simply needs to be moved between the camera and the object. Let's try it again with the lamp in the correct place. Hit ESC to get rid of the rendered image. If not already there, TAB into Object Mode and Hit 1 on the numpad. Select the lamp (Right Mouse Click and move it (G key)) up and to the right. Tilt the scene using the middle mouse button and then move the lamp between the "T" and the camera. Something similar to this.

Step 15: Hit 0 on the numpad, and make sure the "T" is in view. Hit F12 and render the object again. It should be lit reasonable well.

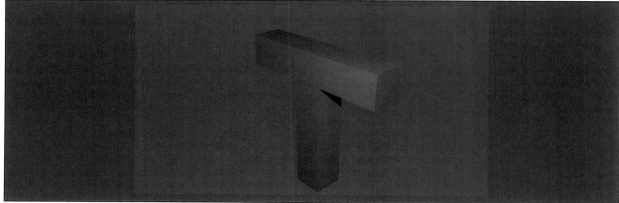

Hit ESC to exit the rendered image.

Exercise # 5 Circle Select (with Extrusion)
Manually selecting multiple vertices (holding SHFT) is something modelers will do for the rest of their lives. However, there is an easier way to select more than one vertex. Making the "T" again is not necessary. For the purpose of practice, only one cube needs extrusion.
Step 1: Go to the top left of Blender, click on File and select New. From here, Tab into Edit Mode, hit 1 on the numpad (front view), and then 5 to get out of Perspective Mode. Finally, hit the A key to deselect the cube.
Step 2: Make sure Limit Selection to Visible is **Off**.
Step 3: Hit the C key and a little dashed circle should appear. Gently scroll the Middle Mouse

Basic Mesh Operations

Button, and take note of the sizing feature. Pick a decent size and place the circle over the top right vertex of the cube, and left click. Move the circle over, and do the same for the vertex at the top left.

Step 4: Hold down the Middle Mouse Button and adjust the view to look at the top of the cube. All four vertices on the top should be selected. If not, and only the front two are selected, Limit Selection to Visible was **On** by accident.

Step 5: Hit 1 on the numpad, then hit E to extrude the box up 2 units.

Exercise # 6 Border Select (with Extrusion)

Step 1: Start with a new scene. Go to the top left, select File, then New. Hit Tab to go into Edit Mode, then the number 1, and 5 on the numpad. Hit the A key to deselect all the vertices. This little priming ritual should be familiar at this point.

Step 2: Make sure Limit Selection to Visible is **Off**.

Step 3: Hit the B key and place the center of the large cross-hairs to the left caddy-corner position (start here). Hold the left mouse button, drag to the right, then down and release.

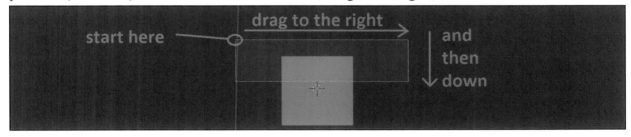

Step 4: Tilt the view by holding the Middle Mouse Button, and drag the mouse down a little. Again, check the top of the cube. All four vertices of the cube should be selected. This 'checking' is a good habit to get into. Occasionally, one or two vertices will accidentally be missed. This is especially true of meshes with many vertices.

Step 5: From here, hit number 1 on the numpad to go back into front view. Extruding can now take place as it did before. Just for fun, extrude up one block, but this time, make it neat by locking the axis (Z key after hitting "E" to extrude).

Exercise # 7 Face Select Mode

Blender allows for a one click selection of an entire face. This serves as a short cut which side steps clicking on each vertex or using circle or border select. However, face selection and vertex selection are not the same thing.

Step 1: Start with a new scene (File → New), but don't hit anything on the numpad; keep the view as it is. Tab into Edit Mode and hit the A key to deselect all the vertices.

Step 2: Click on the Face Select button (it is to the left of the Limit Selection to Visible button). Leave Limit Selection to Visible **On** for this exercise.

3D Modeling

Step 3: The cube should now have little squares in the center of the faces. Fabulous, now an entire face can be selected.

Step 4: Select the top face by clicking on the little black dot in the middle. It should turn orange.

Step 5: Hit E and extrude. Notice that the Blender unit lines are not visible. Hit 5 and then 1 on the numpad to get the grid back.

Exercise # 8 Edge Select Mode

Step 1: Start with a new scene (File → New), then hit X to delete the cube. Go to Add → Mesh → Plane. Keep the view as it is, and tab into Edit Mode. Hit the A key to deselect all of the vertices.

Step 2: Make sure you are in Edit Mode, -otherwise the selection buttons will not be available. Click on the edge select button (next to face select).

Step 3: Right click on the front edge of the plane. See below.

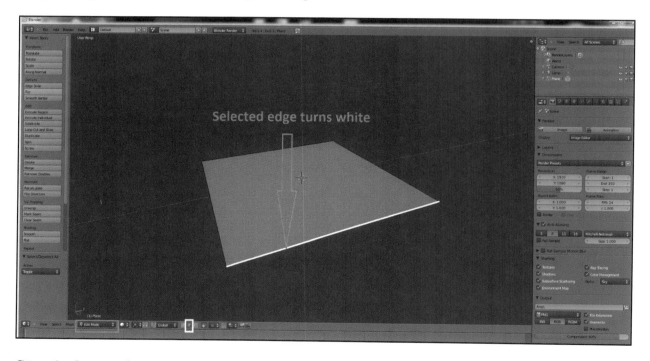

Step 4: Lets make some steps coming up from the plane. With the right edge selected, hit 5, and 1 on the numpad. Hit E to extrude, then Z to constrain the axis and extrude one unit up. Left click to finalize the extrusion. Hit E, then X to constrain the axis, and move over one to the right. Keep repeating this process and build about 5 step and make the final extrusion extended to make the top walkway above the steps.

Basic Mesh Operations

Front View

View titled

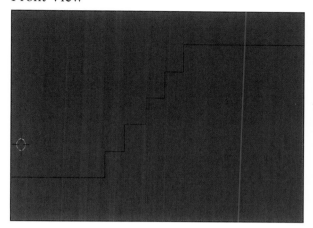
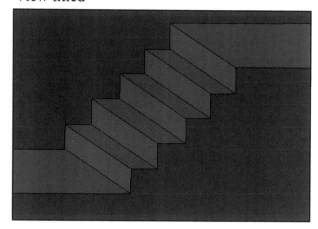

Step 5: Make sure all vertices are deselected (A key).

Step 6: It's render time. Tab into Object Mode and zoom out by scrolling the middle mouse button. The steps have are hardly visible, but they are there. Click on the lamp and position it over to the left. Don't bring it down too close to the steps, as this will over-saturate the steps.

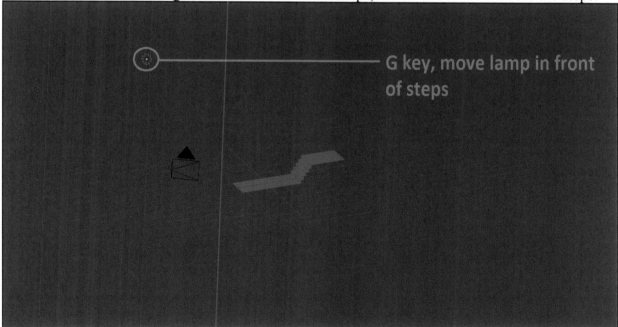

G key, move lamp in front of steps

Step 7: Take the short cut with positioning the camera. Position the steps so that they are in the middle of the screen. Then hit CNTRL + Alt + 0. The camera will position itself to your current view. Hit F12 to render.

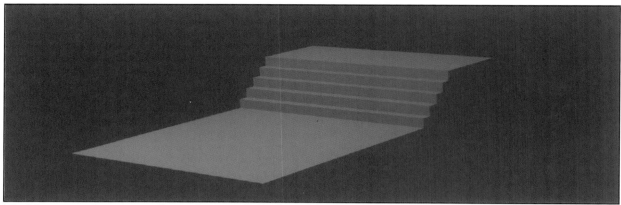

Nothing amazing, complicated, or well lit, but this should start to give an idea as to how easily a city park scene could be set up. With a little coloration, beveling, and texturing, these steps would look VERY nice, not to mention, VERY real.

Exercise # 9 Scaling an Entire Mesh

Scaling and zooming are not the same. Scaling changes the actual size of mesh. Scaling is used constantly in 3d modeling.

Step 1: Start a new scene, hit 5, and then 7 on the numpad, tab into Edit Mode.

Step 2: Place the mouse cursor near the cube, but not on it.

Step 3: Make sure the cube is selected (glowing orange), if not, hit the "A" key.

Step 4: Hit the "S" key and move the mouse to scale.

Step 5: Click the left Mouse Button to finalize the scaling.

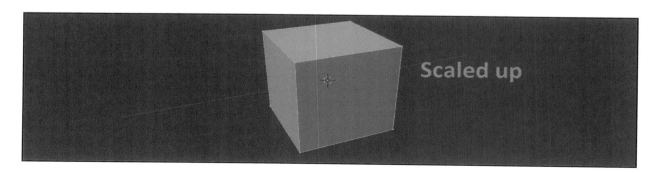

Basic Mesh Operations

Exercise # 10 Scaling Parts of a Mesh

Scaling is not always used to make an entire mesh larger or smaller, but to influence the shape of a mesh's part.

Step 1: Start with a new scene (File → New). Hit X and delete the cube. At the top left, select Add → Mesh → Tube.

Step 2: Tab into Edit Mode and hit the A key to deselect the tube.

Step 3: Make sure that Limit Selection to Visible is **Off**.

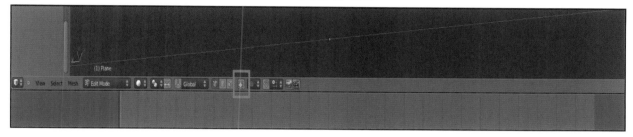

Then hit the B key and select the top vertices. Tip it when done to make sure all the vertices were selected.

Step 4: Select front view by hitting 1 on the numpad. With the top still selected, hit S to scale and drag the mouse outward. Left click to finalize the scaling. This looks like an object which could easily become a car's filter.

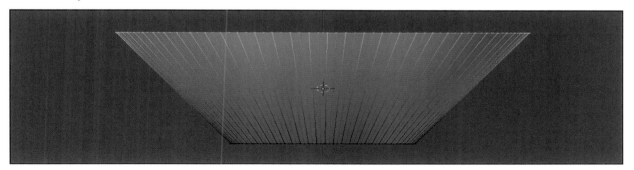

Exercise # 11 Scaling Segments of a Mesh
Step 1: Start with a new scene (File → New), and hit X to delete the cube. Hit 5 and then 7 on the numpad.
Step 2: Go to Add → Mesh → Circle, and at the bottom of the Tool Shelf on the left, put a check beside **Fill** (in the newly appearing properties pane for the circle.) Keep all other settings as default. Tab into Edit Mode.
Step 3: Tap the A key to deselect all vertices. Hold down CNTRL, select the far left vertex and the center vertex.   Hit S to scale and drag the mouse to the right. When done, left mouse click to finalize the scaling.

Left and center vertices selected   Scaled

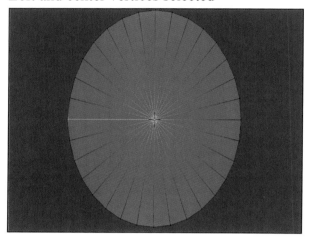 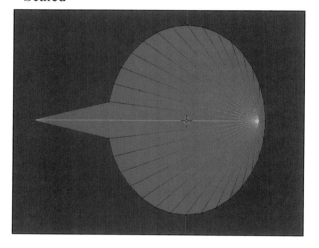

Step 4: Tap the A key to deselect the 2 vertices and hit 1 on the numpad. Now, tap the A key again to select all the vertices of the mesh. Hit E to Extrude, and pull downward. Not much, just a little.

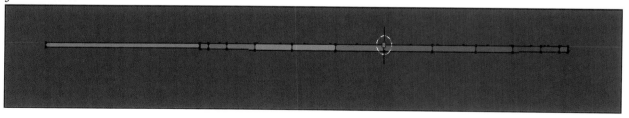

Step 5: What you have made is the tip of a grandfather clock hand. Hit 7, tilt the mesh to make the vertices on the back-end visible and select them with the C (Circle Select) key.

See picture on next page.

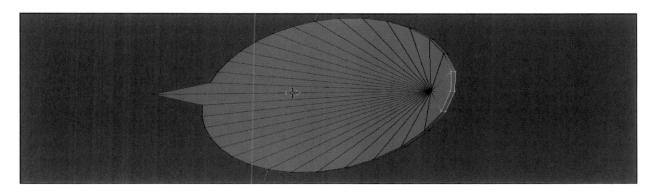

Step 6: Hit 7 again, then E to extrude out the hand. You now have an nice old fashioned grandfather clock hand.

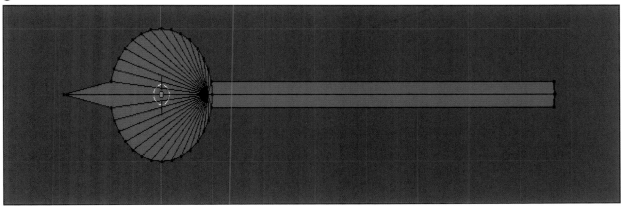

Exercise # 12 Scaling for Flattening
Step 1: Start a new scene, hit X to delete the cube. At the top, go to Add → Mesh → UV Sphere. At the bottom of the Tool Panel, set the segments to 90.
Step 2: Hit 5 and 1 on the numpad and tab into Edit Mode.
Step 3: You are going to make the beginnings of a .45 caliber bullet but not finish it. Turn **Off** the Limit Selection to Visible.
Step 4: Deselect all vertices with the A key. Hit B and select the top part of the UV Sphere.

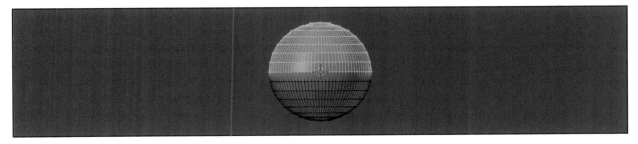

Step 5: Hit E to extrude and drag the cap up.

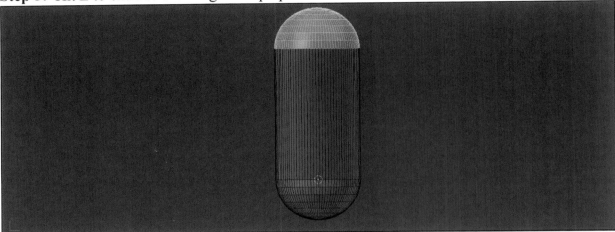

Step 6: Great, but we want to keep one end flat to get the bullet shape. This is easy to do. Tap A to deselect all the vertices and Hit B to border select all of the bottom vertices.

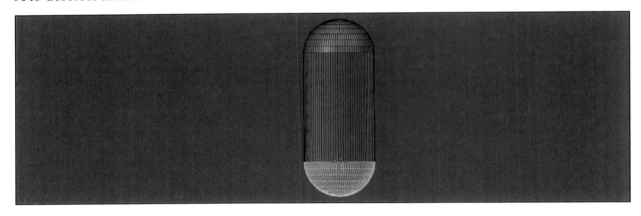

Step 7: With the bottom still selected, hit S to scale, then Z (scaling along the Z axis), then hit 0 on the numpad. The result is shown in the next 2 pictures.

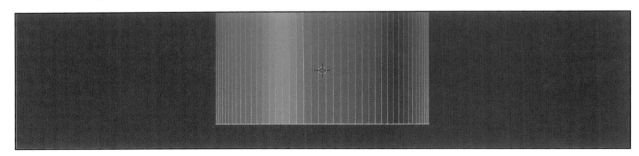

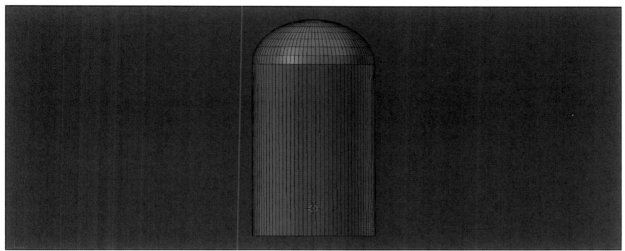

Note: What just happened is that you instructed all the vertices to flatten down to zero with respect to the Z axis. This is a handy little trick to flatten areas of a mesh. It can be used in numerous circumstances.

Note: When entering a value on the numpad after hitting S to scale, Blender automatically understands that a 'scaling value' is being entered, and not a request for the view (e.g., Front, Top, Side). When scaling is finalized, the numpad is switched back viewing options.

Exercise # 13a: Proportional Editing (Roman Spear Tip)

Step 1: Restart Blender, and keep the cube. Tab into Edit Mode and hit A to deselect the mesh. Select the 4 corners of the top face, and subdivide it 4 times. Tap A when done.

Step 2: Turn Proportional Editing **On** by selecting **Enable** and to the right; choose **Sharp** as the falloff type.

Step 3: Of the newly subdivided vertices, select the one in the middle. Hit 1 on the numpad. Hit G and pull the vertex up.

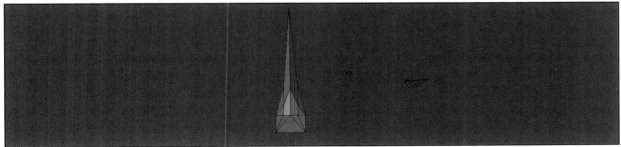

A perfect Roman spear tip. The vertex is not only pulled up, but 'also' the others in immediate proximity. They are pulled proportionally, and hence the name: Proportional Editing.

Exercise # 13b: Proportional Editing (Military Tarp)
Step 1: **Restart Blender** and delete the cube with X. Add a plane and tab into Edit Mode.
Step 2: Hit 7 (numpad), then Subdivide the plane 5 times by hitting W. Tab A when done
Step 3: **Enable** Proportional Editing and to the right, select **Sphere** as the falloff type.

Step 4: As before, select the very center vertex, then hit 1 on the numpad. Hit G and pull the plane up into a dome shape. Without finalizing anything (in other worlds, don't click), scroll the mouse wheel down.

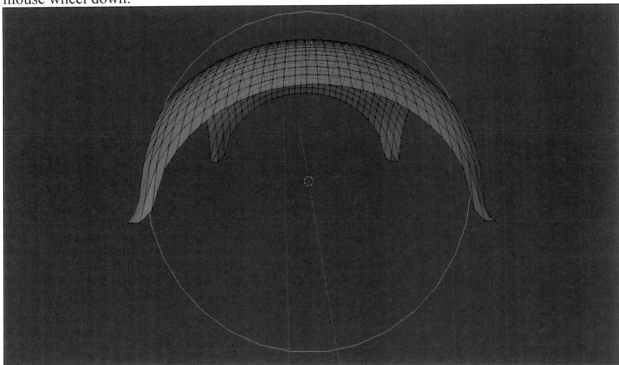

With further tweaking, this could easily become a military tarp with Jeeps or other cargo underneath. It could also be formed into a parachute.

Exercise # 13c: Proportional Editing (Droopy Eyed Monkey)
Step 1: Start with a new scene, and delete the cube with X. Add → Mesh → Monkey.
Step 2: Tab into Edit Mode, hit 7 on the numpad, and turn Proportional Editing **On**. Select **Root** as the falloff type.

Basic Mesh Operations

Step 3: Select the vertex in the picture.

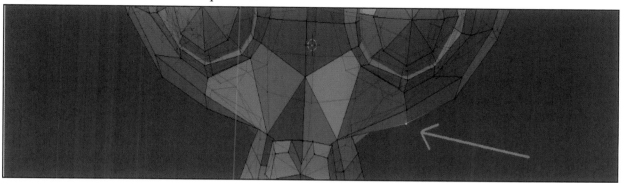

Step 4: Hit G and scroll up on the mouse wheel to make a circle about the same size as what is pictured below.

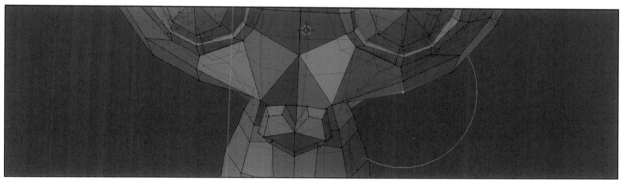

Then pull down a little

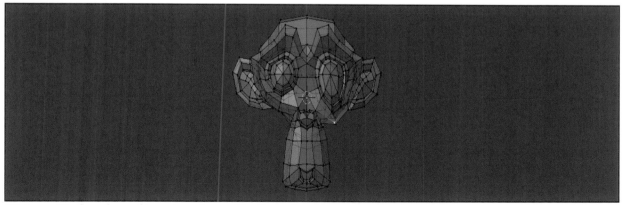

Note: Notice how it not only pulls the cheek down, but also the eyes. An exaggerated, droopy-eyed cartoon effect is produced. This effect is powerful.

3D Modeling

Discussion:

Proportional Editing is something that newcomers tend to shy away from during the early stages. With experience, it will be used as needed. To say that it comes in handy from time-to-time would be understatement. Want to quickly make mountains from a flat plane? How about craters on the moon, or a cement skateboard park with bowls? Proportional Editing transforms what would normally be complex and arduous tasks into exceedingly fast and easy ones. A powerful tool!

Chapter 4: Automated Operations

For mesh manipulation, Blender offers a feature rich environment for making troublesome tasks easier; these come by way of automated operations. This chapter continues on with very short micro-exercises designed to teach techniques without making lengthy, finished models. The idea here is to learn basic modeling techniques, and to not spend hours recreating the work of others.

Exercise # 1 Filling

As happens often with a mesh, an area needs to be filled. Such is the case here.

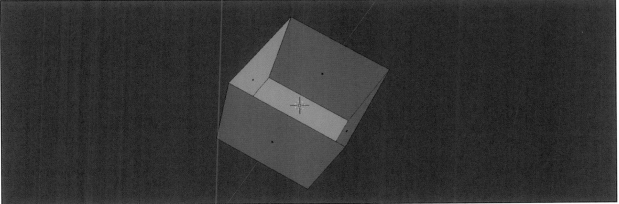

Blender can fill anything with 3 or 4 vertices, but no less and no more. In other words, the 'fill' must result in a triangle or a quad. Filling means nothing more than providing a face where none exists.

3D Modeling

Step 1: Start with a new Blender scene → tab into Edit Mode → deselect the mesh (A key).
Step 2: Select Face Select Mode and select the top face. Hit X and select Delete Faces (not Vertices).

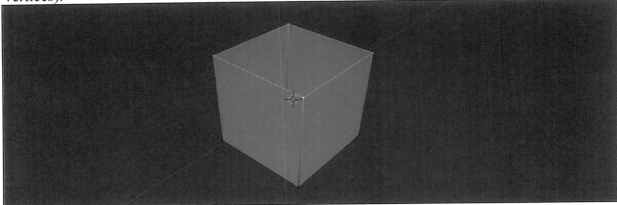

Step 3: Go back into Vertex Select Mode and select all four top vertices. Hold SHFT and click on them.

Step 4: With the vertices selected, hit the F key to fill. That is all there is to it.

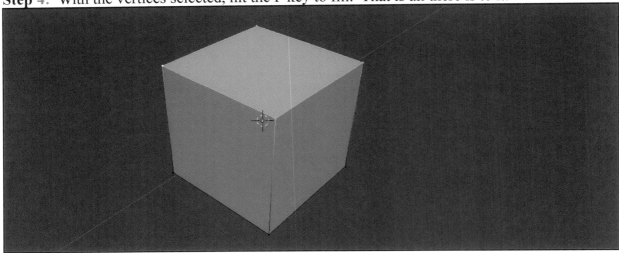

Exercise # 2 Merging Vertices (Pyramid)
Step 1: Start with a new scene and tab into Edit Mode. Deselect all vertices (A key), then hit 5 and 1. Turn Limit Selection to Visible **Off**.
Step 2: Hit the B key, and select the top 4 vertices of the cube.
Step 3: Hit W → Merge → At Center. You now have a pyramid.

Exercise # 3 Merging Vertices (Triangle with Depth)
Step 1: Start with a new scene. Hit 5 and 1 on the numpad. Tab into Edit Mode.
Step 2: Make sure Limit Selection to Visible is **On**.
Step 3: Hit 7 (numpad) for the top view. Hit the B key and select the bottom 2 vertices again.
Note: With Limit Selection to Visible On, only the front 2 vertices will be selected. This is exactly what is desired.

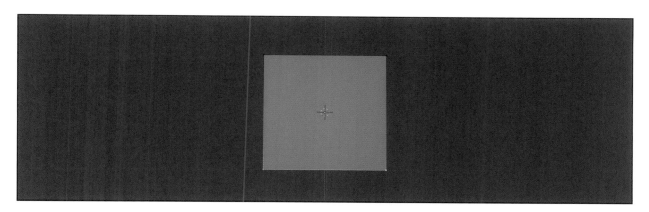

Step 4: While in top view (7 on numpad), hit W → Merge → At Center.

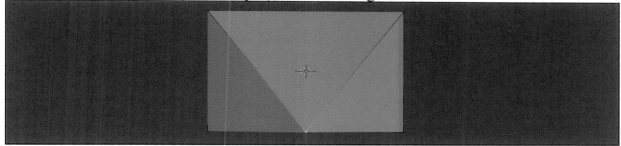

Step 5: Hit the A key to deselect all vertices, and then B. Select the two top vertices.

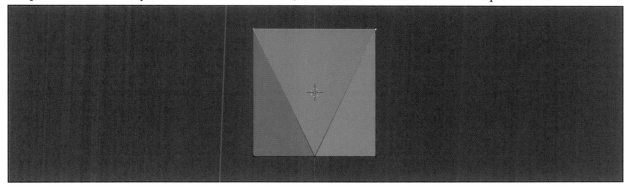

Step 6: Again, W → Merge → At Center.

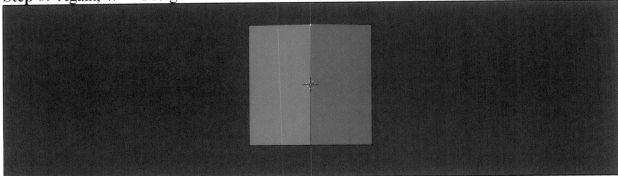

Hold down the MMB and move the scene around. A triangle with depth was made.

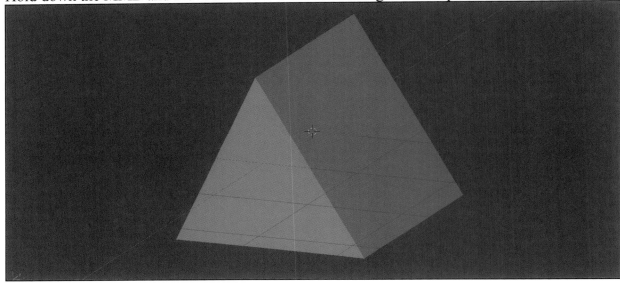

Exercise # 4 Ripping

Merging vertices together is not always desired, but rather, the opposite, -to have them ripped apart. Blender does in fact refer to this process as ripping. For the next exercise, pretend you are making a tutorial, a book perhaps, for origami. However, you don't want to just place dotted lines where the paper is to be ripped, you want to go the extra mile and actually show it being ripped.

Step 1: Start with a new scene, hit X to delete the cube. Add → Mesh → Plane. Hit 5, then 7 on the numpad.

Step 2: Tab into Edit Mode, hit W and subdivide the plane. Do this 4 times.

Step 3: Hit the B key and select the vertices shown in the following picture.

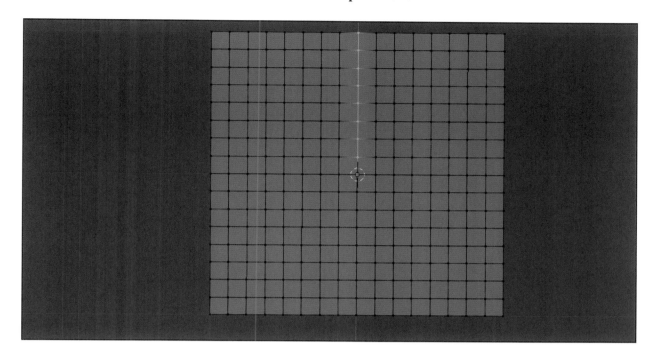

Step 4: Hit V to rip the vertices. After doing so, pull them over to the right to create the rip in the paper. Hit R and slightly rotate the line of vertices (just to make it more pronounced).

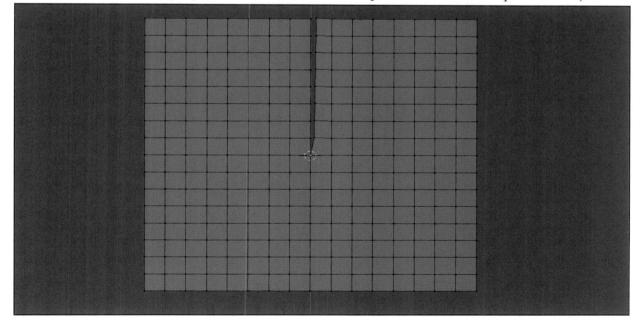

Exercise # 5a Gaining Extra Vertices (Subdividing)
Step 1:   Start with a new scene. Hit X and delete the cube. The go to Add → Mesh →
Cylinder. Keep the default values. Hit 5 and 1 on the numpad, then tab into Edit Mode.
Step 2: Hit S, then Z. Scale the cylinder up 6 units (total).

Step 3: We want to make a flying saucer, but there is a problem. We have very little to grab in
terms of horizontal vertices. Let's subdivide to get a few more vertices. With the entire
cylinder selected, hit W, then select **Subdivide**.

Step 4: Deselect the vertices by taping the A key. Turn Limit Selection to Visible **Off**, and hit
the B key to select the entire middle row of vertices.

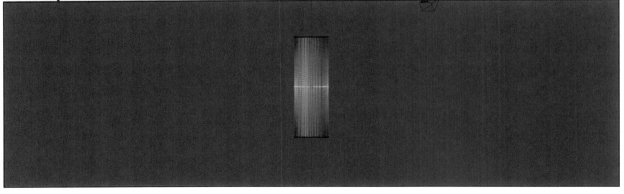

Step 5: Hit S to scale and pull out the middle vertices until a good UFO shape has been
achieved. Your cursor will most likely run out of screen real estate when scaling. This is fine,
just repeat the scaling procedure. Your result should be similar to the following picture.

Automated Operations

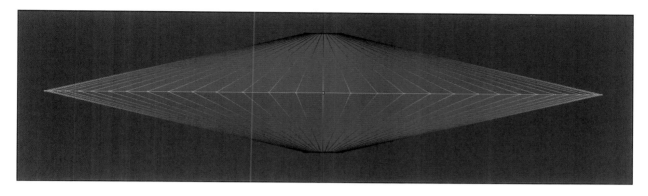

Exercise # 5b Gaining Extra Vertices (General Loop Cut)

Step 1: Start with a new scene, hit X to delete the cube. Then Add → Mesh → Cylinder. Keep the default values. Hit 5 and 1 on the numpad. Tab into Edit Mode.

Step 2: Hit S, then Z and scale the entire Cylinder 6 units high (total).

Step 3: Instead of subdividing, let's use the loop cut. With the Cylinder unselected (also works with the Cylinder selected), and the mouse cursor over it, hit CNTRL + R. A line should have appeared in the middle. Left click, -it will now move with the mouse. Position the loop cut in the center and left click to finalize.

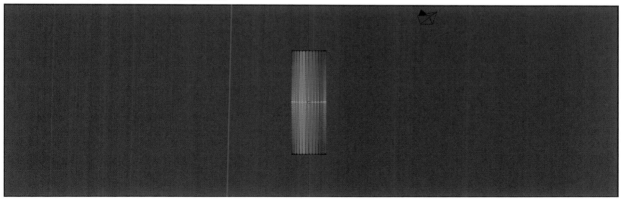

Step 5: Select the newly added loop cut and scale as before. End out with the final UFO shape.

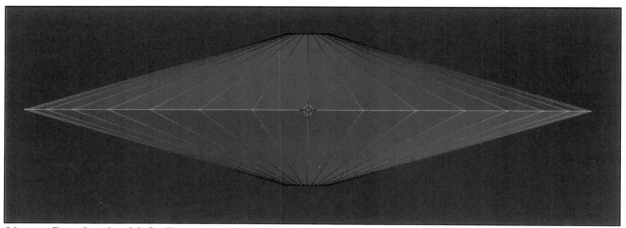

Note: So why do this? Because nothing more than a horizontal loop cut was needed for the outward scaling. Subdividing gives the center loop, but it also increases the number of vertical edges (unneeded). In this case, using the loop cut was the most economical way, by keeping the vertex count lower. This "too many vertices issue" is of no great concern at this point, but it will be paramount when more complex meshes start to develop. Loop cuts have many other uses, especially when it comes to controlling unwanted Subdivision Surface smoothing. More on this subject will be given in upcoming exercises.

Exercise # 6 Gaining Interior Face Vertices

There is a way to gain extra vertices on a mesh's surface (face). Learning this simple procedure is extremely important. Modelers use this technique constantly, not only to gain extra vertices for detail, but also to obtain concentric circles for controlling/shaping purposes.

Step 1: Start with a new scene. Hit X to delete the cube. Hit 5, then 7 on the numpad. Add → Mesh → Plane.

Step 2: Tab into Edit Mode. Hit E to extrude, and immediately Left Click to finalize the scaling. Hit S and scale in the new extrusion.

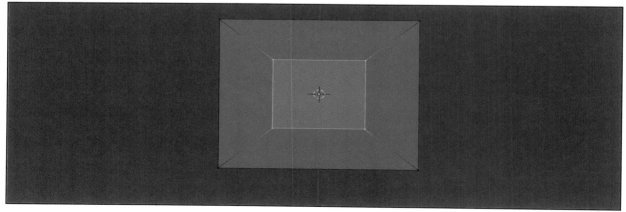

Chapter 5: Connecting Meshes & Parenting

Exercise # 1 Hand Stitching

Step 1: Start with a new scene. Hit X to delete the cube, then hit 5 and 7 on the numpad. Add → Mesh → Circle. Tab into Edit Mode.

Step 2: We want to create another which will be joined to the existing circle. Adding another object while in Edit Mode will make that object editable with the initial one. Move the 3d cursor off to the right (newly created objects appear at the position of the 3d cursor) and add another circle. Add → Mesh → Circle.

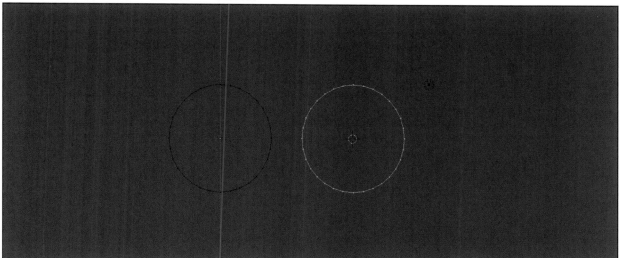

Note: Had the second circle been created in Object mode, it would be a separate object from the first; meaning that both could not be manipulated simultaneously in Edit Mode. Only one could have been selected in Object Mode, and then manipulated in Edit Mode.

Note: Having both circles editable while in Edit Mode could have also been achieved by duplicating the first circle (in edit mode: select it + (SHIFT + D)).

Step 3: These need to be connected in the middle. Select the vertices shown (hold SHFT + Right Click each of them. Then Hit F to fill.

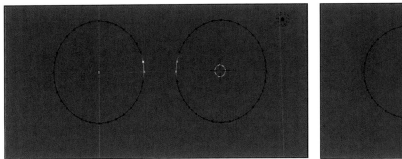
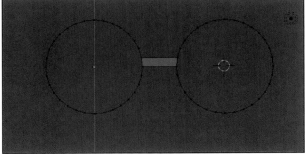

Step 4: Tap the A key to deselect the vertices. Select the 4 vertices show in the picture below. Hit F again, and tap A to deselect when done.

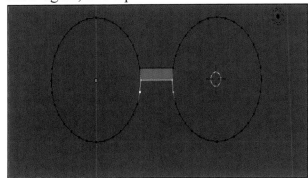
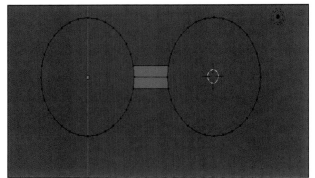

This model could now be the beginning of an old fashion pair of rounded eyeglasses.

Exercise # 2 Merging

Merging isn't only used to collapse vertices to a center point in an existing mesh (remember the previous tutorial which made a 3D triangle from a cube), but it can also be used to connect objects. Let's take a very simple example which illustrates this technique.

Step 1: Start with a new scene, hit X to delete the cube. Hit 5 and 7 on the numpad. Add → Mesh → Plane.

Step 2: Tab into Edit Mode. Left click and place the 3D cursor above the plane. Add → Mesh → Plane.

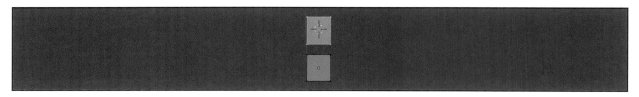

Step 3: Fantastic. Just pretend these are more complicated objects in need of connecting. Say for instance, a finger being connected to a palm, or something similar. Drag the top plane down to where the vertices almost meet. Select the 2 vertices on the left.

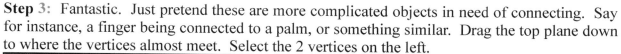

Hit W → Merge → At Center.

Repeat both steps for the vertices on the right hand side.

Exercise # 3 Joining

As repeatedly stated before, when additional meshes are added to a scene, they are typically added in Object Mode. This makes it possible to edit them one at a time by selecting one and hitting tab to enter Edit Mode. This also stops the problem of having one mesh being accidentally interwoven into another. Once that happens, time must be taken to separate them. In the preceding examples, we broke this rule because we knew the newly added mesh would immediately be connected to the initial mesh. The vast majority of the time, additional meshes will be created in Object Mode, then joined later if needed. Once joined, they are, in effect, one mesh which can be edited all at once.

Step 1: Begin with a new scene. Delete the cube with X. Let's make a simple head and place a dunce hat on it. Imagine that these are meshes which have both been worked on separately and now need to be combined into one mesh. Add → Mesh → UV Sphere (the head), Add → Mesh → Cone (the dunce hat). While in Object Mode, grab the cone using G and move it up to the top of the head. Hit R and rotate it. Then hit S to scale it down a bit. See picture.

3D Modeling

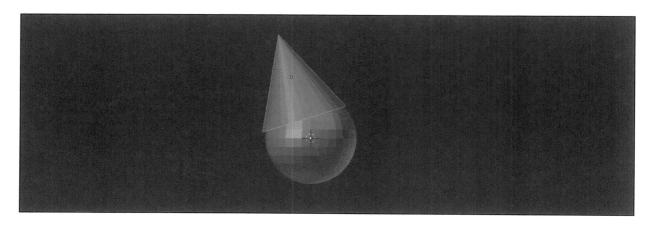

Step 2: With the Cone already selected, hold down SHFT + and Right Click on the Sphere.

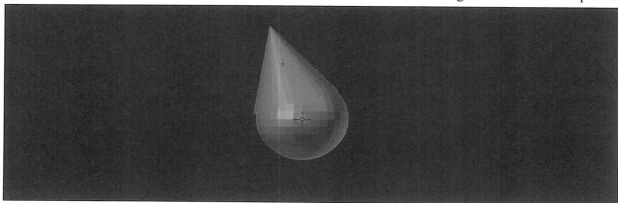

Both objects should be selected.

Hit CNTRL + J to join the meshes and tab into Edit Mode. If everything was done correctly, both meshes will now be one and all vertices should be visible in Edit Mode. See below.

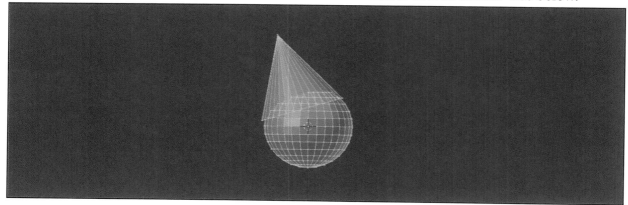

Connecting Meshes & Parenting

Note: Reversing this 'Joining' can be done. Tap A to deselect everything, select the top vertex of the cone (dunce hat), then hit CNTRL + L; this will link every vertex associated with the first selected (in other words, it will select the entire cone (dunce hat). With it selected, hit the P key and choose 'Selection.' This will make them separate objects which can only be edited separately. This procedure is very handy for separating two meshes which have become accidentally intertwined. It is also used for more general purposes.

Exercise # 4 Parenting

Parenting is the process of assigning one or more meshes to another mesh, thee parent. Meaning that, if the parent is moved, the mesh or meshes parented to it will move with it. An example of this would be a Christmas tree with bulbs. It wouldn't makes sense to make the tree and the bulbs all at once. The bulbs would be made separately and then placed. After positioning, you may want to move the tree. This is worrisome because the bulbs would have to be repositioned each time the tree is moved. Parenting allows the bulbs to be moved with the tree, but also allows the bulbs to be moved individually. If any confusion is at hand, this exercise will clear things up.

Step 1: Start with a new scene, and delete the default cube with the X key. Hit 5 and 1 on the numpad as usual. Stay in Object Mode.

Step 2: Add a cone (Add → Mesh → Cone), and add a UV Sphere. Scale the sphere down somewhat. The idea here is for the cone to represent what would be the Christmas tree and the sphere as a bulb.

Step 3: Grab the sphere and place it on the side of the cone. Reference the picture.

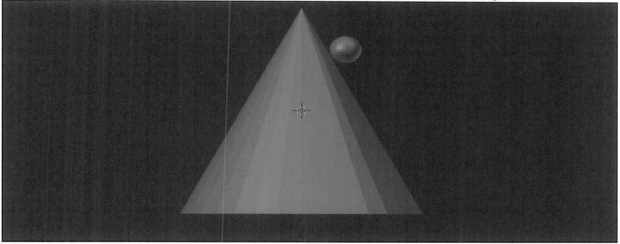

Step 4: Select the bulb first, then hit SHIFT and select the cone. Both should now be highlighted.

Step 5: Hit CONTROL + P and click Object. That is it.
Note: The selection order is important. Always remember, the last one selected becomes the parent.
Step 6: Hit the A key and make sure everything is unselected. Now select the cone and hit the G key to move it. Play around with it. Notice how the sphere moves with it. The cone is the parent, and controls the movement of the child.
Step 7: Hit the A key again and deselect everything. Now select the sphere. Hit the G key and move it. Notice how it moves independently of the parent mesh. This is perfect for any repositioning needs, but the 'parenting' is still maintained.

Chapter 6: Creating Curves

Exercise # 1 Combining Extrude and Scale

Time for some old fashioned training; this is how grandma and grandpa made curves back in the old days. While the manual method for curve creation lacks any kind of new-school automation, it still works. In fact, this method is simpler, faster, and less of a hassle than using the curve modifier.

Step 1: Start a new scene, hit 1 and 5 on the numpad as usual, then X to delete the square. Stay in Object Mode and select a circle (Add → Mesh → Circle). At the bottom left of the Tool Shelf, put a check beside fill.

Step 2: Tab into Edit Mode. The circle should already be selected. Hit E and extrude up a tad. Left click to finalize the scaling. NOT TOO MUCH.

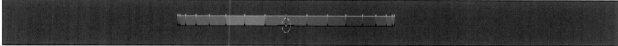

Step 3: After extruding, hit S to scale outward. Left click to finalize the scaling.

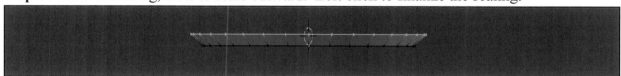

Step 4: Extrude up again and left click to finalize. Hit S to scale, and again, left click to

finalize the procedure. Keep doing this until the shape of a shallow bowl comes out.

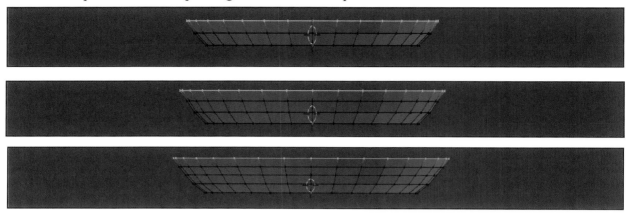

Step 5: With the bowl completed, a little problem is at hand. The top is capped due to the circle being initially filled. Hold down the middle mouse button to tilt the view in order to see the top. Deselect the entire mesh with the A key, and select the very middle vertex of the top cap.

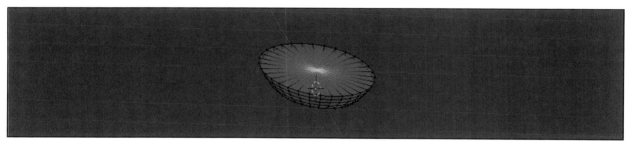

Step 6: Hit X and annihilate that vertex. Congrats, you now have a shallow soup bowl.

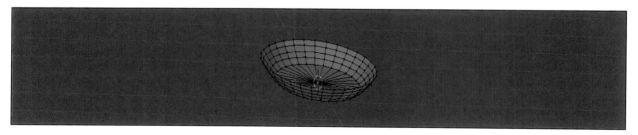

Exercise # 2 Manually Creating Curves from Loop Cuts
Step 1: Start with a new scene, X to delete the cube. Add → Mesh → Tube. Hit 5, then 1 on the numpad and tab into Edit Mode.

Creating Curves

Step 2: With the tube selected, hit S to scale, then Z, and scale the tube into a long pipe shape. It is going to become a cane with a curved handle on the top.

Step 3: Place the mouse cursor in the middle of the tube and hit CNTRL + R. Scroll the mouse wheel up for 2 additional cuts (this will give 3 when counting the center cut).

3D Modeling

Step 4: Tap the A key to deselect the tube. Place the mouse cursor in the top portion of the tube, and hit CNTRL + R again and scroll the mouse wheel for a total of 7 new loop cuts. The idea is to cut it enough times to give some good control for shaping.

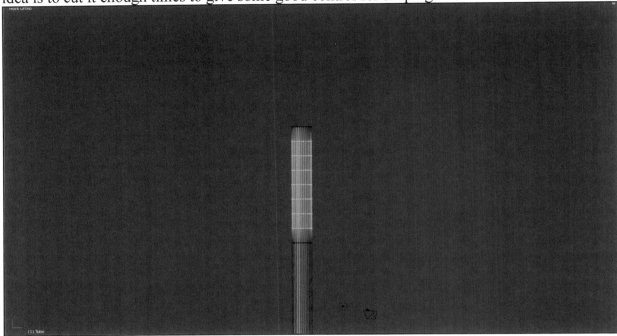

Step 5: Tap the A key again to deselect the loops. Turn **Off** Limit Selection to Visible. Hit B, and select the entire top portion of the cane. Hit R to rotate it to the left, and then G to bring it back into alignment.

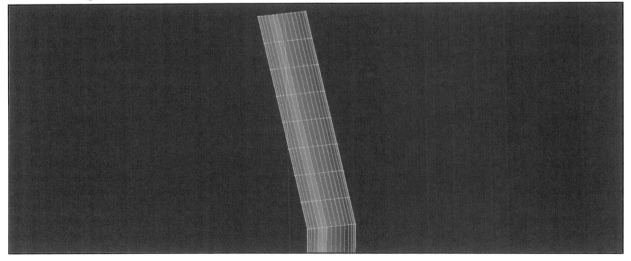

Creating Curves

Step 6: Tap the A key to deselect all vertices. Hit B, and select all the loops, except for the bottom one which is already completed. Repeat the same process of hitting R to rotate, and then G to straighten it out.

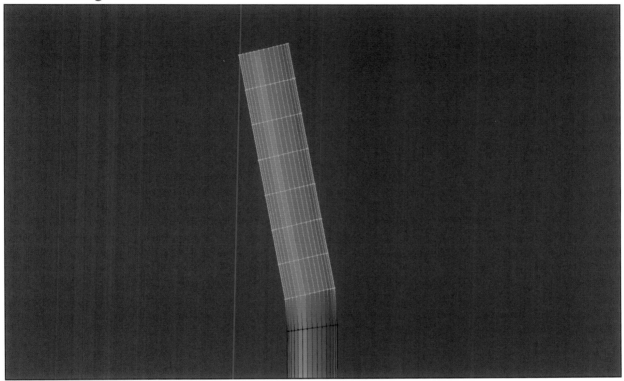

Step 7: Keep doing this all the way up. It may take some finagling, but that is ok. You should eventually end up with something similar to this. It does not have to be pretty.

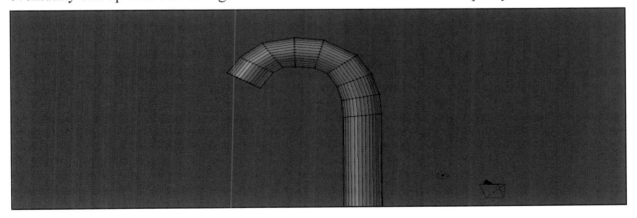

Step 10: Almost done, we ran out of segments. Extrude 2 more down and add some addition loop cuts.

Use (CNTRL + R) to add additional loop cuts in needed areas.

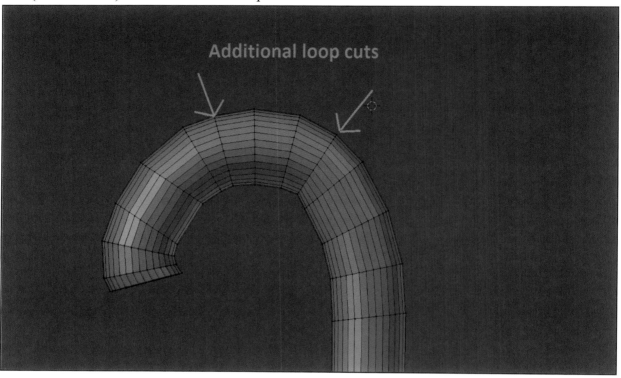

Do nothing more with the model. While far from elegant, the idea was simply to demonstrate manual curve development with loop cuts, and then adding addition loops if needed.

Exercise # 3 Curve Modifier (Automated Method)
      Up to this point, nothing similar to the curve modifier has been demonstrated. The idea is to create a mesh in need of curving, and then to add a curve object. The curve object is then shaped (curved) as desired, and Blender is instructed to have the original mesh to follow the same shape as the the curve object. It is basic mimicry.
Step 1: Lets make a fishing pole which is bent from the weight of having a large prize fish on the line. Start with a new scene, X to delete the cube. Add → Mesh → Tube. Hit 5, then 1 on the numpad, then tab into Edit Mode.
Step 2: Just as before, hit S, then Z and scale the tube upward. Make it long enough to be a fishing rod pole. Tap A to deselect the vertices. Turn Limit Selection to Visible **Off**. Hit B and select the very top loop. Hit S and scale it down to make the tip of the fishing pole. Tap A

Creating Curves

again, hit B, and select the very bottom loop. Hit the S key and Scale it down, but not as much as the tip. See photo below.

Step 3: Then place the mouse cursor in the center, hit CNTRL + R and scroll the middle mouse wheel up to add bunch of loop cuts. Estimate yours to look similar to the picture.

Step 4: Great, the pole is done. Time to add the Curve. Tab into Object Mode, Add → Curve (not Mesh) → Path. Tab into Edit Mode.

Step 5: Grab the little Curve by hitting G, and move it to the left of the rod. Hit R to rotate, then type 90 on the numpad. Hit S and scale it up a little bigger than the fishing rod. See photo.

Step 6: Now left click on the center orange dot on the curve, hit G and pull it out to the left. Do the same for the one above and the one below center. However, don't pull them out as much. Reference the photo for this.

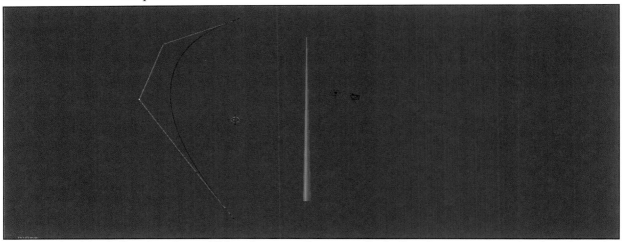

Note: The black line is what will be the actual curve. Only 3 points were manipulated, and a perfect phishing pole shape has been acquired. Blender makes it easy!

Creating Curves

Step 7: Great, almost done. Here is the tricky part. To get the pole to mimic the bend of the path, a Curve modifier must be applied to the pole. Tab into Object Mode. Click on the pole to select it (VERY IMPORTANT). Click on the wrench icon, and add a Curve modifier. The Curve modifier is added to the mesh being curved, not the Curve itself. In the Curve Modifier panel, click on the text entry box for OBJECT, and select **Curve**. The pole should immediately deform.

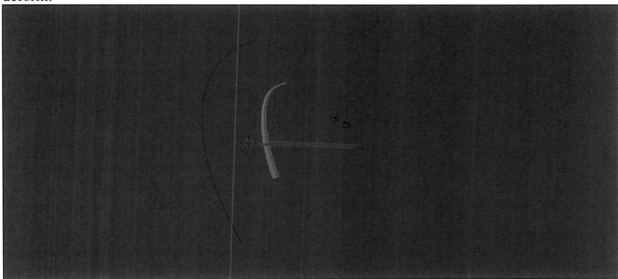

Step 8: Great, it worked, but it lacks a good bend. Nothing like a proper fishing pole. Looks more like a bent sewing needle. Here is the trick. Click on the Curve object and hit G to move it around. It will modify it on-the-fly. A better shape is seen below.

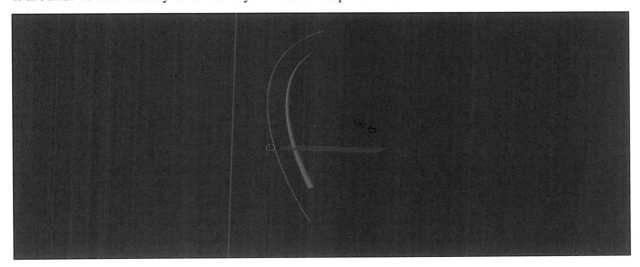

Step 9: To finalize, click back on the pole to select it and click **Apply** in the Curve modifier panel. At this point, the actual curve is no longer needed, and can be deleted with X. What you are left with is a nice fishing pole rod.
Step 10: Duplicate a few lamps with SHFT + D, position the pole, then hit CNTRL + Alt + 0 to position the camera to the current view. Then F12 for a quick render.

Discussion:
     Mastering curves is a fundamental technique in 3d modeling, -one which must be practiced. In the given examples, curve formation was kept as simple as possible, but that in no way implies inferiority regarding the techniques or results. Shaping curves manually can always be done, but in certain situations, the curve modifier comes in handy; this is especially true when curves must be applied to geometrically complex meshes. Making the curve by hand in the latter exercise (fishing pole) would have been painful if it were to be shaped by hand. In this case, the Curve modifier takes care of all the loops in one shot. As a side note, the Path Curve is often times easier for beginners than the Bezier, which relies on complicated, oftentimes troublesome handles to shape the curve.

Chapter 7: Smoothing Meshes

Exercise # 1a Subdivision Surface Modifier
Step 1: Start a new scene and delete the cube with X. Add a UV sphere (Add → Mesh → UV sphere.)
Note: A smooth gray marble is desired and this ugly thing with rough hewn faces just isn't going cut it.
Step 2: With the UV Sphere selected, click the Modifier button (the little wrench icon). In the modifier pane, click on Add Modifier and select Subdivision Surface. For the **View** value, up the setting to 4 and do the same for **Render**. What should be seen is a perfect (or nearly so) ball. This is exactly what is desired. Congratulations, you have successfully used your first Subdivision Surface Modifier.   So what exactly happened?   Blender just did 'a little multiplication of vertices' in an effort to smooth the object.

Step 3: Zoom back out with the middle mouse button.   Position the camera. When happy with the positioning, hit F12 and render the scene. A nice round ball! When finished viewing the round goodness, hit Esc.

Note: The Subdivision Surface modifier is the head honcho, thee Grand Poobah, and raining world champion of smoothing.   There is however another smoothing feature available in Object Mode (under Tools), and shockingly enough, it is called Smooth.   This feature, although appearing by name to take precedence over the Subdivision Surface modifier, is nothing close to it. The Smooth feature is a shading trick with limited effect and does not add vertices.   It is typically used in conjunction with the Subdivision surface modifier. Ignore it for now and simply concentrate on the big daddy, -that is where all the power is at!

Exercise # 1b: Permanency with the Subdivision Surface Modifier

 In the previous example, your first Subdivision Surface modifier was successfully used. You selected a mesh, added the modifier, set the **View** and **Render** levels, and then rendered the scene. This is how most people, beginner and advanced alike, use this modifier. It can, however, be used in a different manner, which allows for the newly added vertices to be manipulated. This is where **Applying** comes in.

Step 1: Start with a new scene, but don't change the view. Tab into Edit Mode.

Step 2: With the cube selected, hit W and subdivide the cube once. Now tab back into Object Mode.

Step 3: Click on the Modifiers icon and add a Subdivision Surface modifier. Turn the **View** and **Render** Values up to 3.

Step 4: Tab back into Edit Mode. Now is the time that you will want to modify the newly created vertices which smoothed your model, however, they are not currently available.

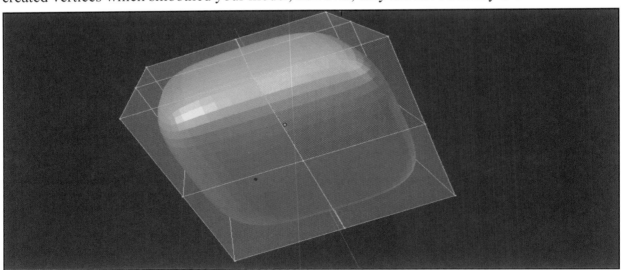

Step 5: Tab back into Object Mode, and click Apply (it's the button above the the **View** and **Render** values in the subdivision Surface pane). The Subdivision Modifier pane just disappeared. The modifications are now permanent and set to the cube. Now Tab back into Edit Mode, and this is what you will see. The vertices can now be manipulated.

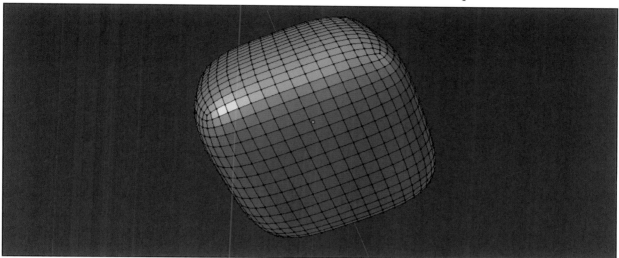

NOTE: Applying the Subdivision Surface modifier is not always needed or desirable. It can at times produce too many vertices, which can make the mesh almost impossible to easily modify. Using it without applying is all that is necessary most of the time. After all, it can be used and rendered without applying. There is a choice here, and the vast majority of the time, the Apply button should not be used! It is however, available if needed.

Exercise # 2 Subdivision Surface Modifier Overindulgence

No, this is not a bug, it is a memory problem and processing issue. The subdivision Surface Modifier comes with a price. Any mesh can be continually subdivided (up to 6x) using this method. For beginners, this modifier is pretty much like the gas pedal on a 911 Porsche. More, more, and more, can get you into hot, hot, hot water. Every-time a Mesh is moved or spun, the CPU is constantly redrawing it on the screen. It has to do a mathematical calculation for every vertex. With every subdivision comes a massive increase in vertices, and when abused, real time mathematical processing bogs down. This generally is not a problem with one small mesh (provided that your system is powerful enough), but with a whole scene, even the fastest systems can be brought to a halt, or crash.

Step 1: Let's stress your system. Start with a new scene. Hit X and delete the cube. Go to Add → Mesh → Monkey. Tab into Edit Mode.
Step 2: Go to the Modifiers tab → Add Modifier → Subdivision Surface Modifier. In the pane, turn the **View** and **Render** values up to 6.

Step 3: First, hold down the middle mouse button the move the mesh around. It should be slower and lag. Second, hit F12 and render the scene. A noticeable increase in render time should be observable.

Imagine if multiple meshes were in the scene with 'cranked up' Subdivision Surface modifiers applied to all of them. The system could not handle it, and a crash would most likely occur. Imagine also if these meshes were being used for an animations. If it takes that long to render a single image, how long would it take for a full movie? As for video games, especially 3D games, this becomes critical.

Exercise # 3 Subdivision Surface Modifier with Unexpected Results
Step 1: Start a new scene, but stay in Object Mode.
Step 2: The cube is fine for this example. Make sure it is selected and click on the modifier icon (wrench). Click on add modifier and then Subdivision Surface. What happened? Our nice square turned into a very rough ball. This is a warning! While subdividing a surface is very handy, it can (at times) result in very dramatic shape changes.
Step 3: Let's fix this. First of all, when you created the new Subdivision Surface modifier, a pane opened up. On the right of the pane, there is an X. Click it, and remove the modifier.
Step 4: Tab into Edit Mode, and make sure the box is selected (A key). Hit W to bring up the specials menu and select subdivide (not subdivide smooth). Do this 3 times. Please note, subdividing while in Edit Mode and the Subdivision Surface Modifier are two completely different things.
Step 5: Tab back into Object Mode and select the modifier icon (wrench) and Add Modifier. Again, select Subdivision Surface Modifier. Much better! A nice square, with smoothed edges.

What exactly happened? By subdividing the object, you created controlling loops which limit the influence of the Subdivision Surface Modifier. More will be shown on controlling loops in chapter 7.

Exercise # 4a Smooth Vertex (Line)
The Smooth Vertex Button in Edit Mode is a little more intelligent than people assume. It modifies angles in an effort to increase smoothness. For some angles, which are more out of whack, it will have a greater effect. This simple exercise demonstrates this.
Step 1: Start with a new scene and immediately tab into Edit Mode.
Step 2: Tap A the (key) to deselect the cube. Hold down shift and right click on all of the vertices except one. Hit X and delete vertices. You should be left with one little vertex. Fabulous!
Step 3: Hit A to select the lone vertex and hit E to extrude. Make a curved shape with multiple

extrusion. Something in the shape of a skateboard ramp. But there is a catch, grab and pull out 2 vertices, as to disrupt the smooth flow of the ramp.

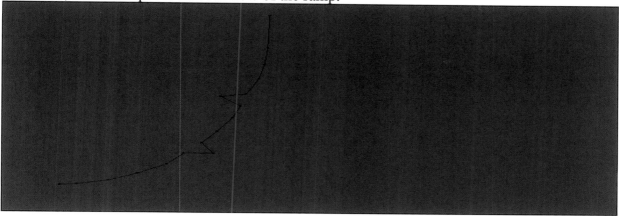

Step 4: Great, hit the A key to select the mesh and start hitting that Smooth Vertex button over in the tool shelf. Keep hitting it until it is all smoothed out. Something close to this should be the result.

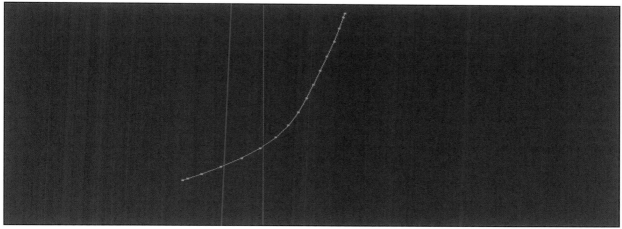

Exercise # 4b Smooth Vertex (Icosphere)
    The Smooth Vertex tool will not work with all types of geometry!
Step 1: Start a new scene. Hit X and delete the cube. Add → Mesh → Icosphere.
Step 2: Tab into Edit Mode, and with the icosphere selected, start hitting the Smooth Vertex Button. Nothing happens, it only gets smaller.
Note: The Smooth Vertex tool works by reducing the angles, but does so in relation to all the other angles. In this case, it has no where to go (in terms of angular reduction). The icosphere gets smaller, but is not effectively smoothed.

Exercise # 4c   Smooth Vertex with Undesirable Results

In certain situation, applying smooth vertex will work, but it unfortunately changes the general shape of the mesh and creates undesirable results.

Step 1: Start with a new scene, hit X to delete the cube. Add → Mesh → Monkey.

Step 2: Hit 5 and 7 on the numpad, and tab into Edit Mode.

Step 3: Make sure the monkey is selected (which it should be by default) and hit the Smooth vertex button. Keep hitting it and notice how it smoothed out the angles. Notice how it also changes the shape when done too much. The below pictures show the total destruction of the original shape. For most modelers, even hitting it once creates too much change. The Smooth Vertex button is only valuable in certain situations.

Default monkey

Smooth Vertex causing strong deformation

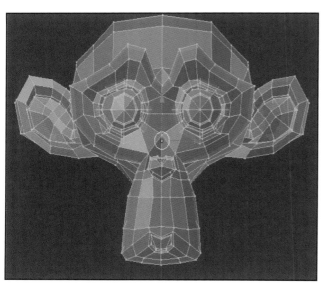 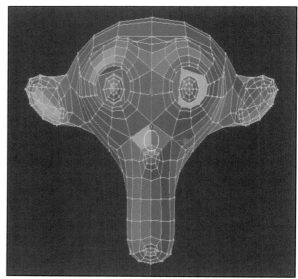

Exercise # 5 Smooth Shading

There is another smoothing button which does not increase the vertex count, Smooth Shading. While not doing any miracles for exceedingly bad geometry, it is still valuable, not to mention, impressive. Unlike Smooth vertex, Smooth Shading is available in both Edit and Object Mode.

Step 1: Start with a new scene, hit X to delete the cube. Add → Mesh → Monkey. Hit 5, then 7 on the numpad and tab into Edit Mode.

Step 2: Select the monkey, then hit the Smooth button in Mesh tools (the panel off to the left).

NOTE: Make sure that the SMOOTH VERTEX button is not hit. There are two buttons in the Mesh Tools panel with the name 'Smooth,' pick the one under shading.

Smoothing Meshes

Step 3: Tab into Object Mode to look at the model without the vertices showing.

Default monkey

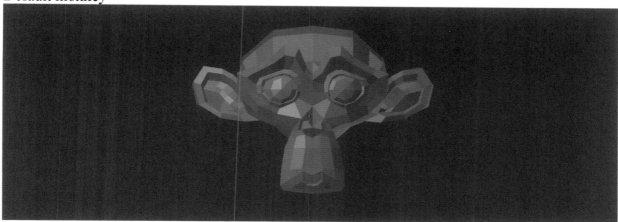

With smooth shading

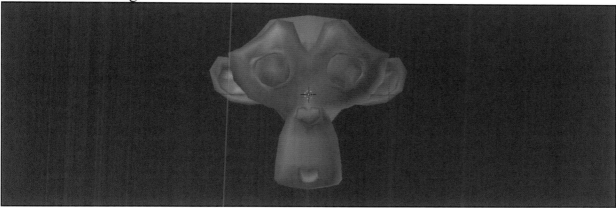

Discussion:

As mentioned before, the Subdivision Surface modifier is the king of smoothing, but increases the computational load. Smooth vertex and Smooth Shading are free in terms of increasing geometric price, but compare poorly to the Subdivision Surface Modifier.

At times, modelers will do nothing more than add a subdivision surface modifier and crank it up. This works well for single meshes that are small. This does not work well for animations, large meshes, scenes with multiples meshes, not to mention video games. When modelers need to be conscious of vertex counts, using Smooth Shading in conjunction with a Subsurface Modifier is good idea. Here are some quick examples to look over.

3D Modeling

Render of default monkey, Vertex count: 507

Render of monkey with Subdivision Surface Modifier at 4, Vertex count: 126,290

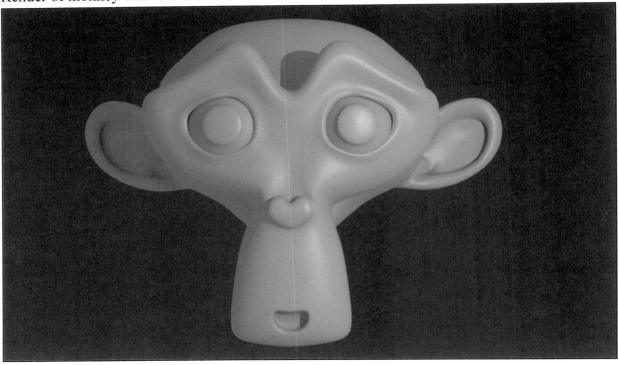

Smoothing Meshes

Render with Smooth Shading + Subdivision Surface Modifier at 3. Vertex count: 31,658

Note: Using Smooth Shading allowed for the Subdivision Surface modifier to be reduced by a value of one. This saved 94,632 vertices, and produces a result on par with the Subdivision Surface Modifier set at 4.

Chapter 8: Controlling loops

Warning: When control loops are added by hitting CNTRL + R, they do not always show up without some finagling. Blender has problems when figuring to add them horizontally or vertically. If encountering such problems (which will most likely occur) move the mouse around on the mesh, especially near the outer areas of the mesh. They should eventually appear. In the following models, only horizontal loops will be utilized.

Exercise # 1 Adding "Controlling Loops" to Fix Subdivision Surface Reductions
Step 1: Add a new scene, hit X to delete the box, and add a Tube (Add → Mesh → Tube). Use the default settings.
Step 2: Great, we now have a Tube, but it is a little rough around the edges. Stay in Object Mode and hit 1 and 5 on the numpad. Go over to the wrench icon, and add a new Subdivision Surface Modifier. Set the **View** and **Render** values to 3.

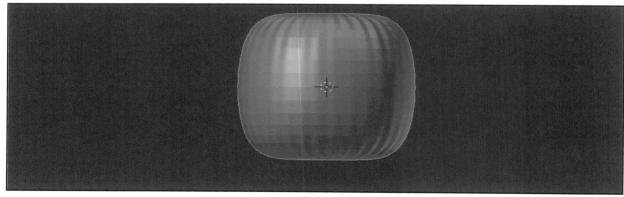

Note: Great, it started smoothing everything, but the desired shape is that of a Japanese style tea cup. The bottom is fine, but the top needs to be relatively flat (with a slight bevel). That is ok, it can be fixed. Pay very close attention to this next series of steps. This technique is used constantly for reducing unwanted smoothing from the Subdivision Surface Modifier.

Step 3: Tab into Edit Mode. Place the mouse cursor over the model. Hold CNTR + R, obtain a horizontal loop, -then immediately left click. The once purple loop, now yellow, can be slid up and down. Slide the loop almost all the way up to the top of the tube.

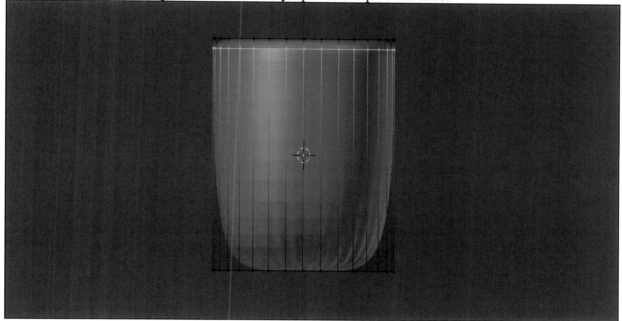

Note: These controlling loops work wonders. They help out time and time again.

Exercise # 2 Adding Multiple Controlling Loops and Edge Slide
Multiple controlling loops can be added in one step. After doing so, the edge slide feature can be used to move the loops.

Step 1: Start a new scene, keep the cube, and add a Subdivision Surface modifier; set the **View** and **Render** values to three. Hit 5 and 1 on the numpad. Tab into Edit Mode.

Step 2: This time we want to make a flask shape. Yes, a flask, as in chemistry class, but what we have is a ball shape. Both the top and bottom are going to need a controlling loop, which could be added one-by-one, but why not just add both at once. Place the mouse cursor in the middle of the mesh and hit CNTRL + R, obtain a horizontal loop, and scroll up the middle mouse wheel up once. *Note: As stated before, this may not show up at first. If the controlling loops do not become visible, move the mouse cursor off to the left or right edge of the mesh.* Left click to finalize the loops and tap the A key to deselect everything.

3D Modeling

Step 3: Hold down ALT and right click on the lower loop, the entire loop will turn orange. In the Tools panel, find the Edge Slide button and click on it. Move the edge down and left click to finalize.

Step 4: Tap A to deselect all the vertices. Hold down ALT and right click on the newly made top loop. Again, hit the Edge Slide button over in the Tools panel. Drag the loop up, roughly the same as the bottom. See next page.

Step 5: Tap A to deselect everything. Turn Limit Selection to Visible **Off**. Hit B and select all the top vertices. Then hit S to scale them down into a beaker shape.

Top Portion Selected

Scaled down

 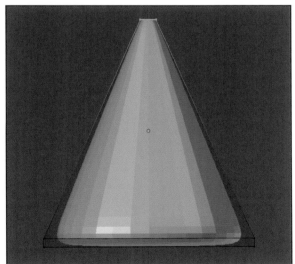

Note: The previous example is somewhat odd considering that it would have been faster just to add each loop one at a time. However, there will be times when adding multiple loops comes in handy. Sometimes, a large number are required.

Chapter9 : Handling Difficult Transformations

Exercise # 1a Making Circles From Non-Circular Topology (Smoothing Method)
Step 1: Start with a new scene, delete the cube with X, then Add → Mesh → Plane.
Step 2: Hit 5, then 7 on the numpad.
Step 3: With the plane selected, repeatedly Hit W and subdivide 4 times.
Step 4: Tap the A key to deselect all vertices and hit the B key to select the inner most box of 9 vertices. Hit X and delete the vertices.

Selected

Deleted

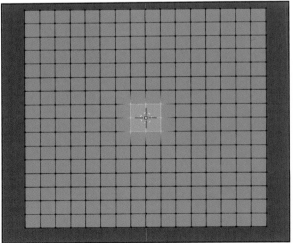
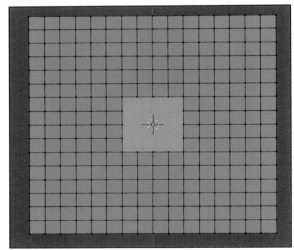

Step 5: Hit the B key and select the box, and then continuously hit Smooth Vertex until the vertices stop moving.

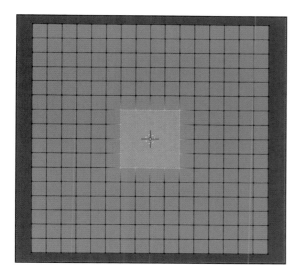 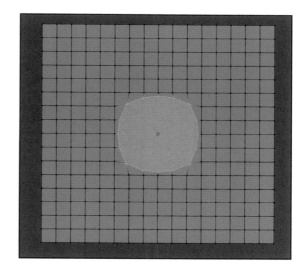

Step 6: Great, the handy Smooth Vertex button has made a circle from a square, but it is unfortunately poorly shaped. Here is the trick to make it more circular. Hit E to extrude, then immediately hit S to scale it into a tight circle. Left click to finalize. Then start hitting the Smooth Vertex button again. Keep hitting it until a well shaped circle is formed.

Extruded and scaled in (scale yours tighter)   Smooth Vertex applied n times

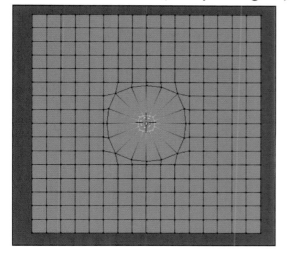 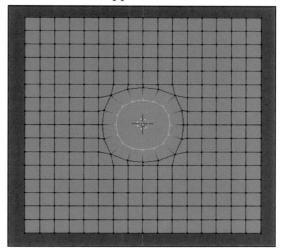

Note: This worked because the surrounding geometry was more circular than the original square. When performing this procedure (for a circular effect), it must be scaled in close to the center point. This allows for the Smooth Vertex tool to be applied more times, which results in a more accurate circle shape.

3D Modeling

Exercise # 1b Making Circles From Non-Circular Topology (SHFT + ALT + S)

Blender has a nice automated feature which will place non-circular arrangements of vertices into a circular shape. The great intricacy of this feature is that it allows for varying numpad value inputs. In other words, you can make a perfect circular form, a ¾ circular form, or a form which is just slightly rounded off.

Step 1: Start with a new scene, hit X to delete the cube. Add → Mesh → Plane. Hit 5 and 7 on the numpad. Tab into Edit Mode.

Step 2: Hit W and subdivide the plane. Do this 4 times.

Step 3: Tap the A key to deselect all vertices.   Hit B and select the innermost box of vertices, then hit X and delete the vertices. See picture.

Selected   Deleted

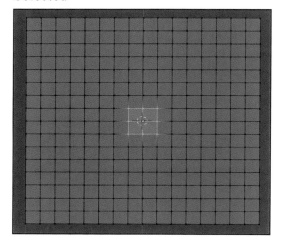
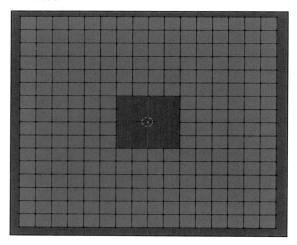

Step 4: Hit B, and select all the vertices which make up the inner most box, and then hit SHFT + Alt + S, then hit 1 on the numpad. Left click to finalize. Ta-dah, a circle.

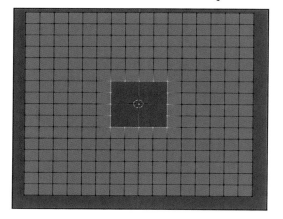
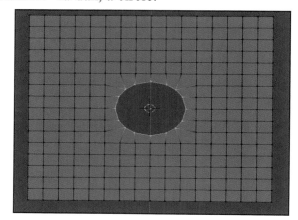

Step 5: Let's take a step back. Hit CNTRL + Z and go back to the square.

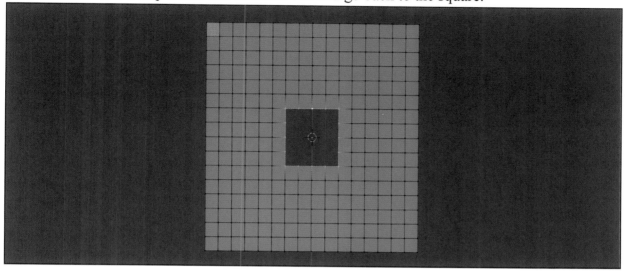

Hit SHFT + ALT + S, then hit .5 on the numpad. This gives you a shape which is 50% square, 50% circle. Which is exactly what would be expected.

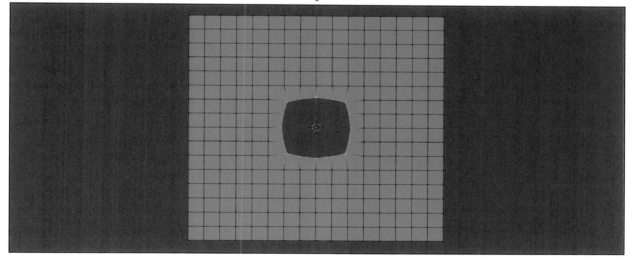

Exercise # 2 Making Circles From Non-Circular Topology (Sphere)
The prior examples worked, but they will not work when trying to make holes in curved meshes. If the Smooth Vertex technique is used in that situation, it will flatten out the area around the curve. This is bad. See picture on next page.

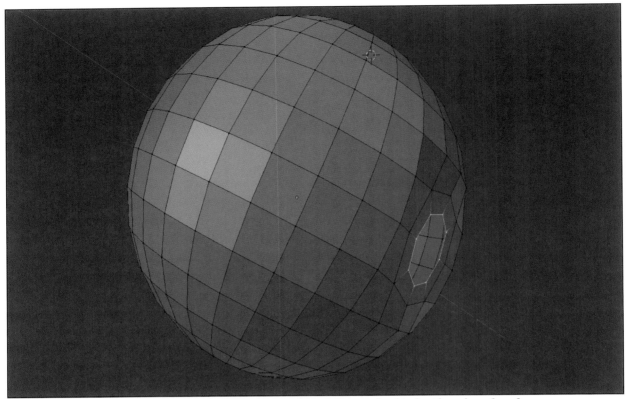

NOTE: SHFT + Alt + S also fails, as it produces irregularity in the circular form.

Modelers typically use the Shrinkwrap modifier to get around these problems. However, this is a beginners book and it is best to learn manually. This manual technique requires a little more work, but is actually easier for beginners to get their head around. And with this method, tools are never needed.

Step 1: Start with a new scene, delete the cube with X. Add → Mesh → UV Sphere. Immediately hit F6. Double the values for the Segments and Rings: 64 and 32 respectively. That pop-up window via F6 is the same as the one at the bottom of the mesh tools. Just another way to get at it.

Step 2: Hit 5, then 1 on the numpad and tab into Edit Mode.

Step 3: What is needed now is to select an area on the mesh where the circle is going to be. Hit the A key to deselect all vertices. From the 3d cursor, select the vertices to make a 16 face square which is centralized by the 3D cursor.

Note: This may be hard to understand. Reference the next 2 pictures.

Hold down SHFT and select them one-by-one. When done, hit CNTRL + E and select Mark Seam. Tap the A key again, and a red seam should be marked. This is nothing more than a reference.

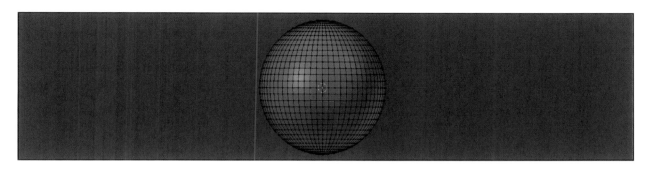

Step 4: Count all the outer vertices which make up the square. There are 16 vertices. Fantastic. We now need a circle with the same number vertices. This will keep the topology nice and clean when everything is connected. Stay in Edit Mode when creating the new circle, but make sure the UV sphere is unselected (this is important). Add → Mesh → Circle. Immediately hit F6 and change the vertices to 16. Hit R to rotate, then Z, then 90 on the key pad. Left click to finalize. Scale down the circle to fit in the square.

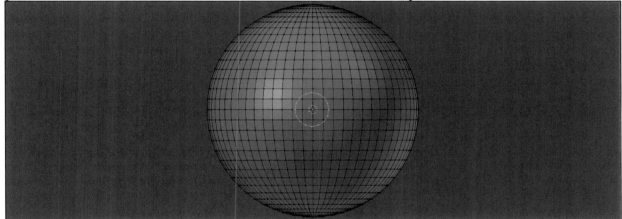

Step 5: Hit 3 on the numpad, then G to grab and move the circle out to the very edge. You want it to be touching.

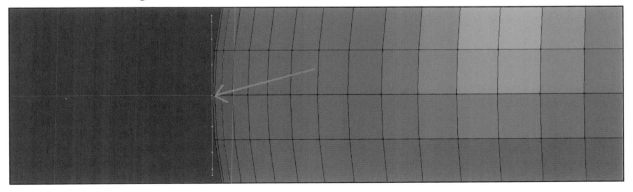

Step 6: Here is the trick. Hit A to deselect all the vertices. Each vertex must be selected one-by-one using the G key, and set flush to the face.

This is the procedure for the first vertex:

Select the first vertex   Hit 3 on the numpad   Hit G, then Y and move flush

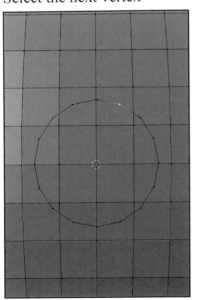

This is the procedure for the second vertex:

Select the next vertex   Position the view for a side shot   Hit G, then Y and move flush

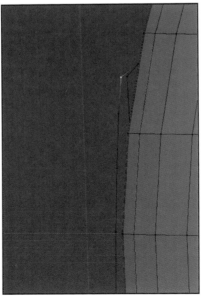

Handling Difficult Transformations

That is it, just keep working your way around the horn. Keep it neat! When finished, this should be the result. It is a very good result considering that it was done manually!

Finished result viewed from the front.

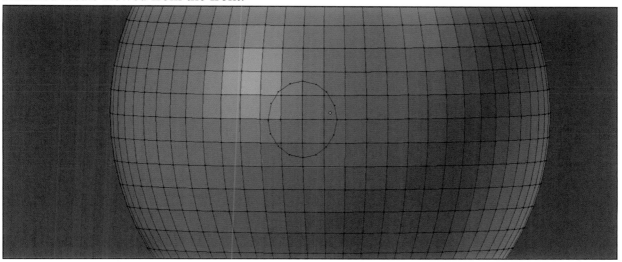

Finished result viewed from an angle.

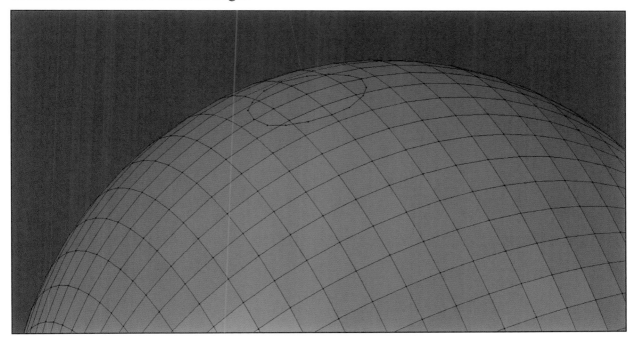

3D Modeling

Step 8: The hard part is over, it is all free sailing from here. Hit 1 on the numpad, select all the vertices inside the circle, hit X and delete them.

Selected   Deleted

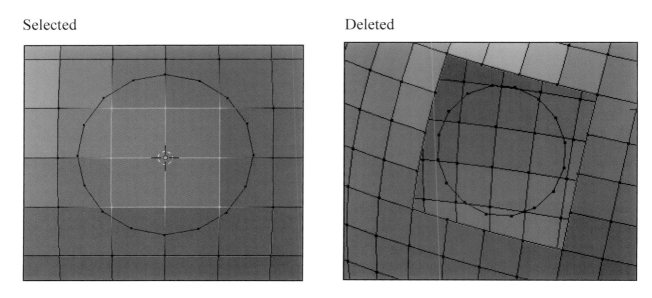

Step 9: We are going to connect the circle to the UV sphere by filling in quads one-by-one. Simply follow the pictures.

Hold SHFT and right click these 4 vertices.   Hit F to fill.

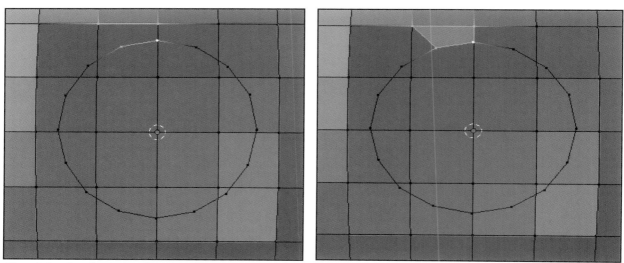

Tap A to deselect the face, and repeat with the next one over.

Next 4 vertices selected

Hit F to fill

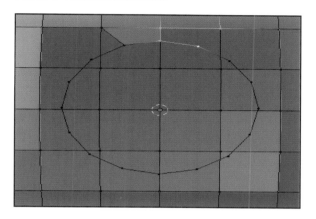 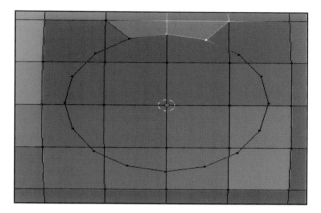

Keep going all the way around the horn in the same manner. The final result should look as such.

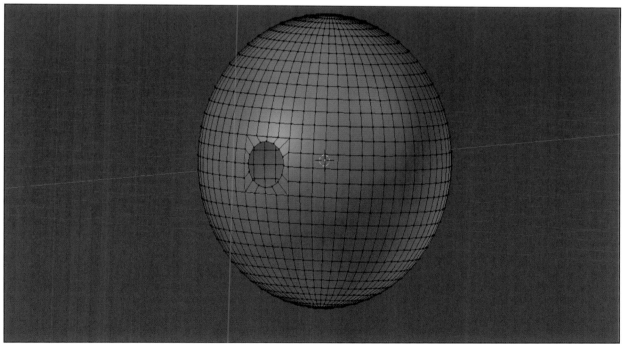

Note: Be mindful, especially with future projects, when connecting one mesh to another, it is VERY advantageous to have the same number of vertices for the connecting areas. It creates clean, problem free topology. Always count the number of surrounding vertices and have the newly added mesh follow suit.

3D Modeling

Exercise # 3 Transitioning From Square to Circular

     This is a fun little exercise. Beginner modelers always have problems when trying transitioning from square to circular. This is very easy to do. Let's make a long, square rod which tappers off to a circular shape.

Step 1: Start with a new scene, hit 5, then 1 on the numpad, then tab into Edit Mode.

Step 2: Turn Limit Selection to Visible **Off**.

Step 3: Select the cube, hit S, then Z and make the cube about 12 units high.

Step 4: Place the mouse cursor roughly in the middle and add 12 loop cuts (CNTRL + R, then scroll mouse wheel). Tap A to deselect when done. Add 4 vertical loop cuts, then tap A. Hit 3 on the numpad and add 4 more vertical loop cuts on the side, then tap A. The pictures follow the progression:

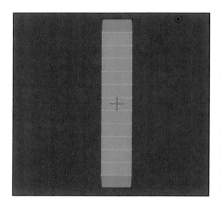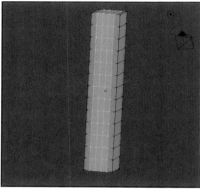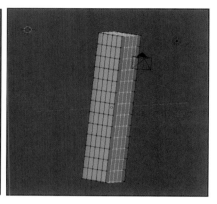

Step 5: Hit 7 on the numpad. Hit B and select the inner box of vertices (make sure Limit Selection to Visible is **Off**) and hit X to delete.

Inner box selected

Deleted

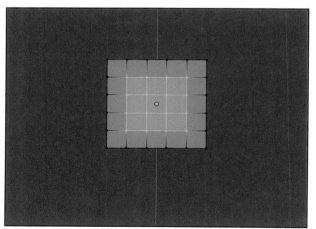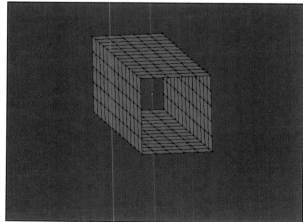

Step 6: Hit 1 on the numpad. Here is where the magic happens. Each of the following loops (numbered 1-5) is going to be turned into a circle using SHFT + ALT + S, with each being given a unique numpad value.

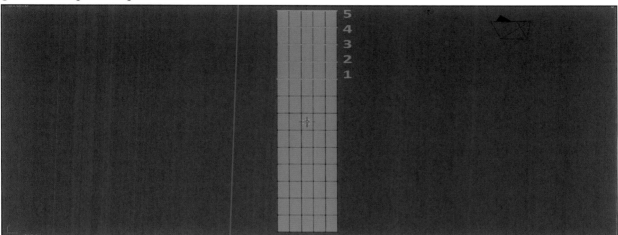

Step 7: Count down, and start with number one. Hit B and select it (Don't select other loops). Then hit SHFT + ALT + S, then .2 and hit the return key to finalize. Hit the A key to deselect once finished. Repeat this procedure for loops 2-5, but give them rounding values of:
loop 2 = .4   Loop 3 = .6   Loop 4 = .8   Loop 5 = 1.

This stepped graduation results is a very smooth transition from square to circular.

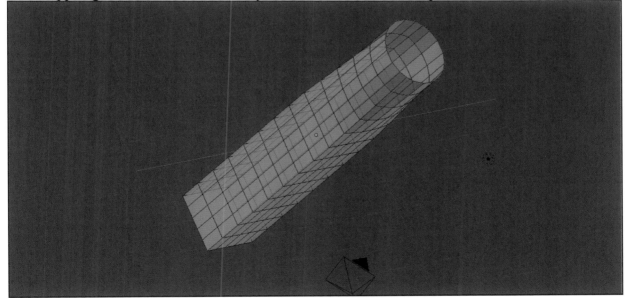

Note: Anything can be done from here, try capping off the end.

3D Modeling

Discussion:

As logic would follow, the next exercise would be transitioning from round to square. The "SHFT + Alt + S, then numpad" method does not work in reverse. Circular geometry cannot be made less circular. It is always best to make the square part first, then circularize it. The only other option is to add in extra meshes and connect them.

Chapter 10: Symmetrical Modeling

Exercise # 1 Symmetrical Modeling (the Spin Tool)

Step 1: Start with a new scene. Hit X and delete the entire cube. Go to Add → Mesh → Plane.

Step 2: Tab into Edit Mode, then hit 5, and 7 on the numpad.

Step 3: Tap the A key to deselect the plane. Hit the C key and select any three vertices. Then hit X to delete them. One vertex should be left.

Step 4: Find the single vertex and click on it. Hit G and move it to the 3d cursor position (dead center). This position is critically important because the spin tool uses the 3d cursor as the spin point.

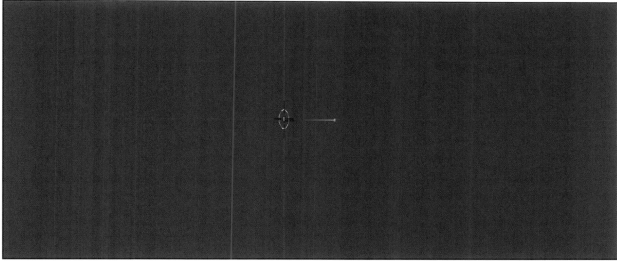

Step 5: Half of a chess piece is going to be made. Hit E to extrude, and move out to the right. Keep extruding little by little and form half of a chess pawn. At the top, stop on the green line. The progression is as follows:

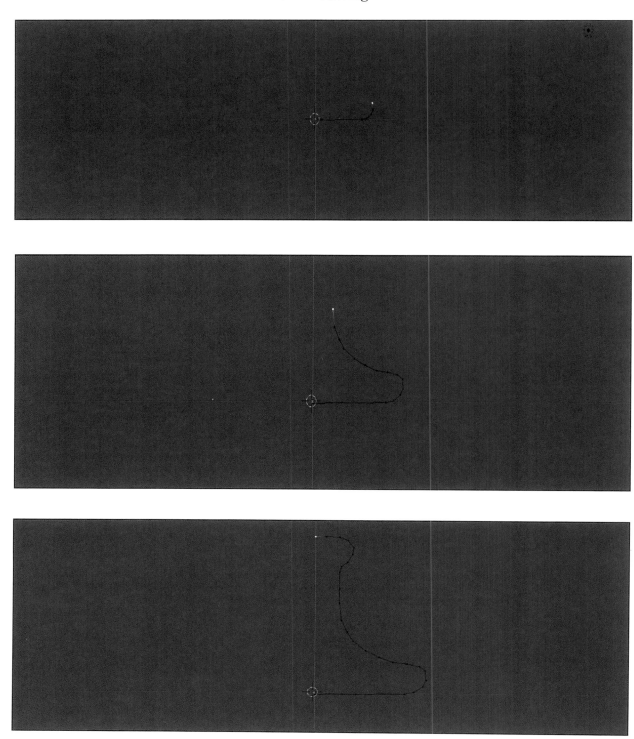

Symmetrical Modeling

Step 7: Hit A to deselect the last vertex at the top and tap A again to select the entire mesh. Hit 1 on the numpad. Nothing much will be visible except a straight line with vertices.

Step 8: Go to the Mesh Tools panel on the left. It should be open by default. Go down the list until the Spin button is found, and click on it.

Step 9: Your mesh should have spun 45 degrees. Hitting the spin button also did one other thing, it opened another box at the bottom of the Mesh Tools panel. Go to it and left click on the entry space for **degrees**. Type in 360 and hit return.

NOTE: The other entry field, listed as steps, increases the smoothness of the spin by adding in additional geometry. Keep the default settings.

Step 10: Hit number 7 on the numpad. There should be a beautiful pawn to be seen.

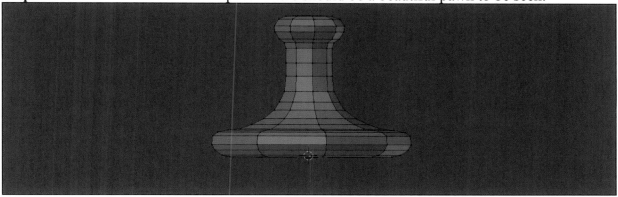

Wait, not exactly beautiful, now is it? This is the problem when it comes to the spin tool. It is hard to estimate proper proportions, and unless yours was perfect, -some scaling is in order. For starters, mine is too squat. I need to scale it up on the Y axis. This is the result.

Note: Yours may have turned out differently and may need to be scaled differently. For example, yours may be too wide. If needing to scale it down, it will have to be scaled on both the X and Y axis. This is done not by hitting X and Y after hitting S to scale, but rather, by excluding the Y axis. Hit S to scale, then SHFT + Y. Don't continually hold it.

Step 11: Tab into Object Mode, Hit the Smooth button in the Mesh tools, and add a new Subdivision Surface modifier. Set the **View** and **Render** values to 3. Go to to World icon (shaped like a little globe) and put a check beside Ambient Occlusion. Set the Factor to .15.

Step 12: With top view selected, hit CNTRL + ALT + 0 to set the camera to the current view. Click the Render icon, set the resolution to 100%. Then F12 to render.

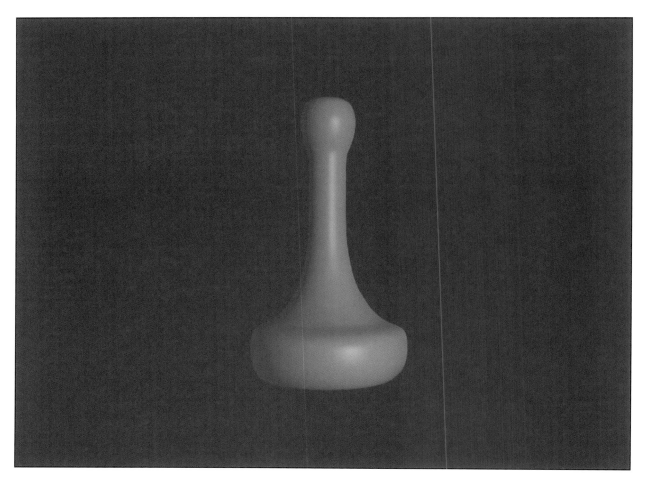

Note: Not a bad result considering that little was done with lighting, and nothing with colorization or textures. A simple setup.

Symmetrical Modeling

Exercise # 2a Symmetrical Modeling (the Mirror Modifier)

The Mirror modifier allows modelers perfect symmetry while demanding half the work. This little gem comes in handy for complex symmetrical meshes; without it, certain jobs in modeling would be excruciatingly difficult. Again, perfect symmetry is given, with half the work! When modeling cars, human bodies and the like, the advantages are easy to see. A boon to the modeling process to say the least.

Step 1: Start a new scene, X to delete the cube and add a plane.

Step 2: Tab into Edit Mode, then hit 5 and 7 on the numpad.

Step 3: With the plane selected, hit W and subdivide the plane. Do this 3 times total. Tap the A key to deselect the plane.

Step 4: Select the left had rows of vertices, and delete them.

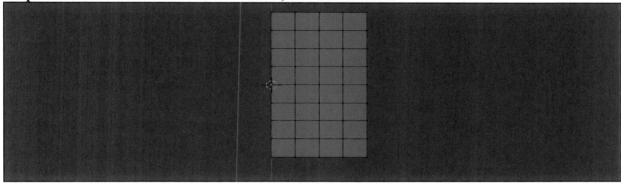

Step 5: Select the entire plane and click the wrench icon (over on the right). Add a mirror modifier. In the mirror modifier, there is a triangle icon button for viewing in Edit Mode, click on it. Also, make sure clipping is checked.

Note: Clipping stops vertices from going over the center line.

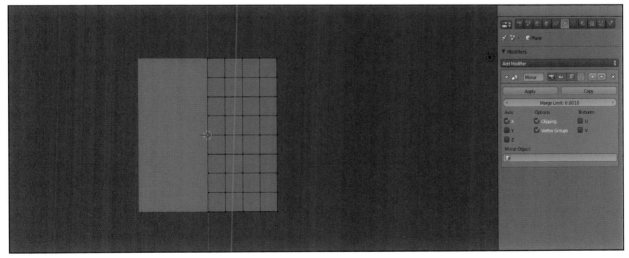

Note: The Mirror Modifier selects the X axis by default.

Step 6: We are now going to make a short sleeved shirt, with the sleeves being made first. Follow the pictures below.

Select the three vertices

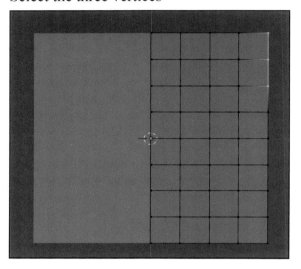

Hit R, rotate a little, then left click

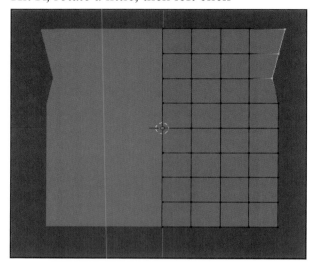

Hit G and pull out to the right a little

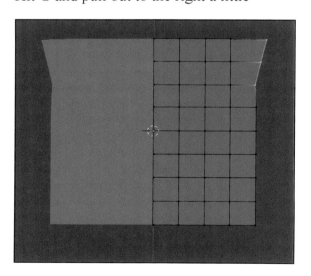

Extrude (E) the sleeve and Rotate (R) a little

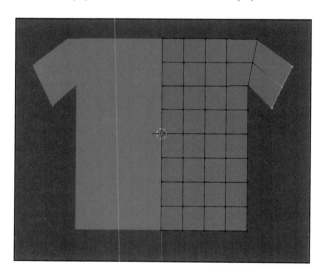

Step 7: Everything looks fine, but the shirt is far too wide. Here is a little trick. Make sure Clipping is checked in the Mirror Modifier. Select the entire mesh, Hit S and scale until one full row of squares gets overlapped. Line them up perfectly! See next picture.

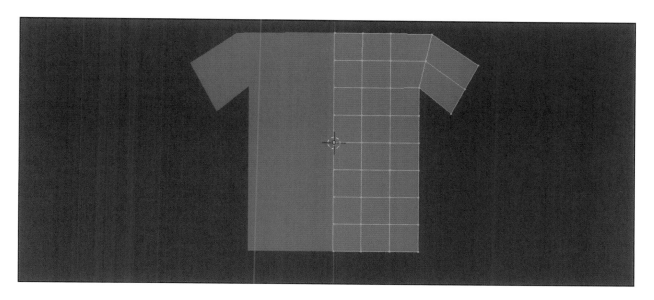

Then Hit W and select remove doubles. If the vertices were properly overlapped, a little pop-up should appear saying that 9 vertices were removed.

Step 8: Much better, -it's starting to look like a proper T-shirt. Follow the next few steps for a nice curved neckline.

Select 2 vertices (B key)

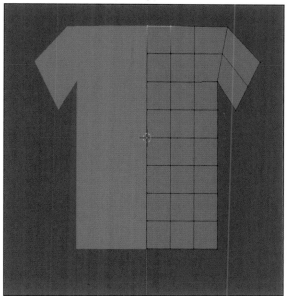

Subdivide 3 times (W key)

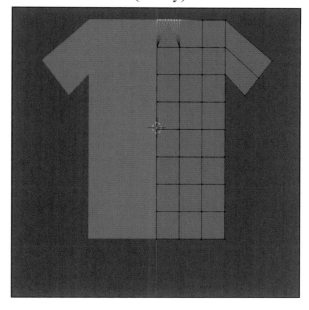

Step 9: Tap the A key to deselect the vertices, and starting at the right, select them one at a time and move them into a curved shape. Perfection is not needed.

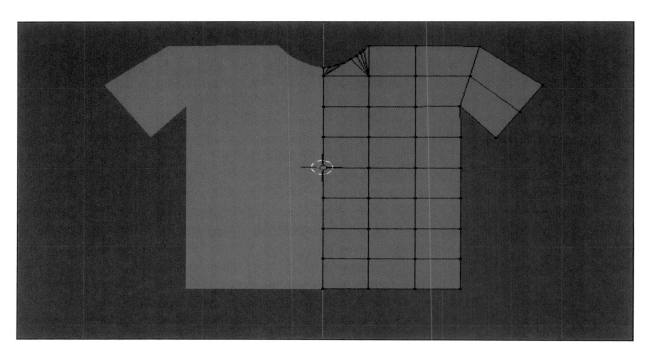

Step 10: Tab into Object Mode and click Apply on the Mirror Modifier. It is all one mesh now. Tab back into Edit Mode, hit 1 on the numpad and hit A to select the entire T-shirt. Hit E to extrude, and give it a little depth, -not too much.

Step 11: Render it out with F12.

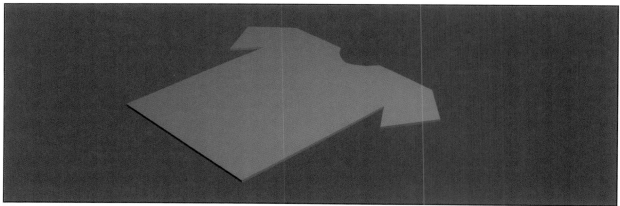

Note: This could easily be sitting on a bed in a popular modern day cartoon. You know the ones, where they purposefully keep the models ultra simple.

Symmetrical Modeling

Exercise # 2b Symmetrical Modeling (Mirror Modifier with Multiple Axes)
Step 1: Start a new scene, X to delete the cube, then 5 and 7 on the numpad.
Step 2: Add a circle, Tab into Edit Mode, and hit A to deselect the entire Mesh.
Step 3: Hit B to border select all of the vertices in the photo. Hit X to delete.

Selected (B key)   Deleted (X key)

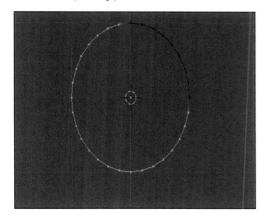 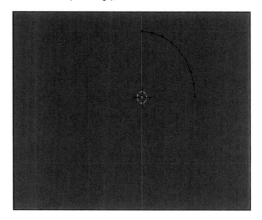

Step 4: Click on the wrench icon, and add a mirror modifier. In the mirror modifier, there is a triangle icon button for viewing in Edit Mode, click on it. In addition, click Y under axis, and make sure clipping is checked.

Step 5: One at a time, click on each of the vertices shown in the picture and hit E to extrude each one to the center. Click apply in Object Mode and the mirror will become permanent. Leave it at that. Nothing fancy was made, but again, the idea is to demonstrate procedure.

3D Modeling

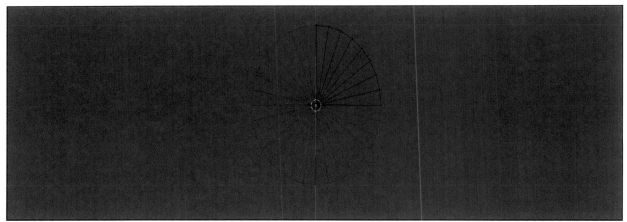

Note: This technique can also be done in 3d (e.g., using spheres). Feel free to experiment.

Chapter 11: Reference Images

Using background reference images for modeling is perhaps the greatest single advantage in increasing realism. Why? It's all an issue of ratio, and correct ratio being important for realism. Try modeling human hands without a picture; it is incredibly difficult. Without a great degree of artistic talent, or a lot of practice, maintaining the correct ratio is almost impossible. The same goes for human faces, cars, buildings, animals, and so on. Get one or two areas of the mesh out of ratio and the realism goes out the window.

For this example, we are going to keep it incredibly simple and demonstrate this technique using a fork. Generally speaking, most modelers will use 3 or more pictures when modeling certain real world objects. Only a top and side view will be used will be used for this example.

Note: When taking pictures of models, the different views have to line up (this will be understood as the fork is modeled). In order for this to happen, pictures must be shot from the same distance, and centered. If a modeler does not have perfectly lined up images, then he or she will have to guesstimate certain areas. This is an annoyance, but more importantly, creates a chance of decreased realism. Keep this in mind. If anything is unclear, the following exercise should clear things up.

3D Modeling

Exercise # 1a   Background Image Modeling (Fork Setup)

Warning: This tutorial is more involved than the previous tutorials, and far more lengthy.

Step 1: Grab a camera or borrow one (webcams are fine). Take pictures (top and side view) of a fork. Be sure to keep the same distance from each, as this will make positioning easier. Make sure the prongs of the forks are pointing in the same direction as the pictures below, as these orientations will be used.

Step 2: Begin with a new scene, tab into Edit Mode, then 5 and 1 on the numpad. Hit X to delete the cube.

Step 3: In the very top right had corner of the viewport is a little white (+) sign and right above it, 3 little lines.

DON'T CLICK ON THE PLUS SIGN! Place the mouse pointer over the three lines, and a cross-hair will appear.

Reference Images

Once the cross-hairs appear, hold down the LMB and pull a new window downward. The top screen should be about 1/3 of the bottom size. It can be moved by placing the mouse over the border, and holding left click.

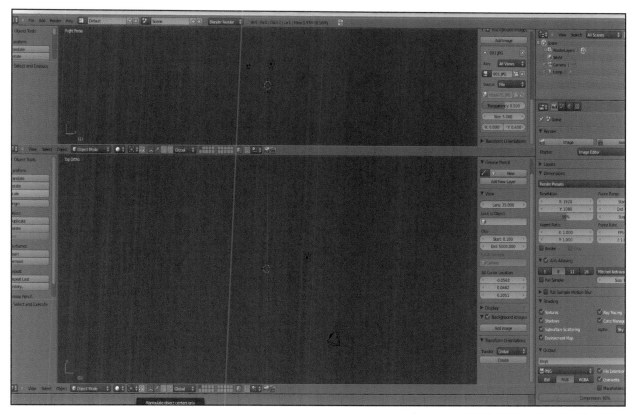

Step 4: For the bottom screen, hit 7 on the numpad, and for the top, number 3. For each, make sure they are both in orthographic view.

NOTE: The images which are about to be loaded will not show up in perspective view.

♦91♦

3D Modeling

Step 5: Place the mouse cursor in each window (viewport) and hit N on the keyboard. Once that is done, start with the bottom screen. Scroll down (in the right pane that N brought up) until **Background Images** is found. There is a little check-box to the left of the name; it must be checked for background images to be seen.
-Hit the small downward facing arrow key to the left of the check-box.
-Click the arrow to the left of Not Set, and then click the Open button.

Using the file directory, find the image Fork, click on it, and click the open button in the top right. Hint: The directory folder with the back arrow may be useful in finding the image. Repeat this procedure for the top viewport (or screen) and load the side image of the fork. *Note: Blender will sometimes place the first loaded image in the other views for background image. If one is already there for the 2nd, then it did in fact duplicated it. This seems to happen intermediately. If so, delete it by hitting the X, and load the correct image.*

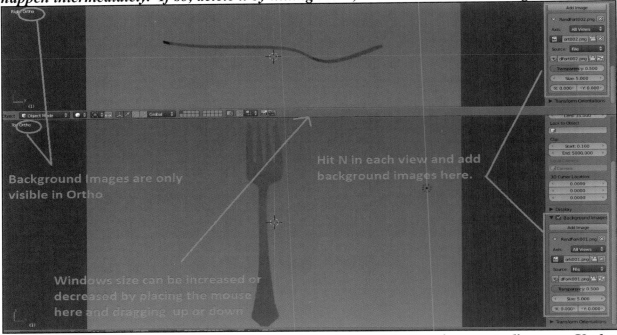

Note: Generally speaking, the idea is to get the top and bottom images to line up. Under background images, where the image was loaded, there are X and Y coordinate values which can be shifted. Normally, we align the first image on the 0, 0 coordinate and the top follows suit. Also, when taking pictures, slightly different depths will create items which are of different sizes. It is normally important to size the image in Blender units for the first image, then adjust all other pictures to be sized the same. There is a size value under background images. While we are not doing any of this for this tutorial, it will almost certainly be needed for future modeling with background images.

Reference Images

Exercise # 1b Background Image Modeling (Fork Modeling)
Step 1: (In the bottom screen) Add → Mesh → Plane, then tab into Edit Mode. To the right of where it says Edit Mode, switch to Wireframe. This little trick makes tracing the image easier, as it allows for increased visibility. Hit A to deselect the plane, then select the top 2 vertices, and delete them. All that should be left is a line. Scale it down as in the picture below.

Selected   Deleted   Selected   Scaled

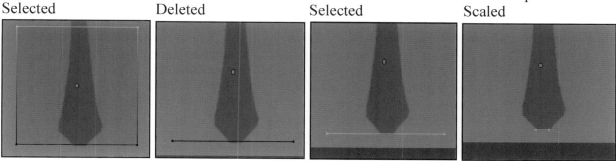

Step 2: From here, the whole idea is to hit E to extrude up and then S to scale. You may need to Hit G to grab and adjust left or right occasionally. Here are the first series of extrusions and scalings.

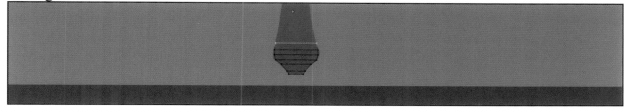

Step 3: Keep going up along the fork, but stop before you get to the prongs. Here is a hint, the areas with the most bending in the fork will need the most extrusions to keep it smooth. Stop when you reach the very beginning of the prongs.

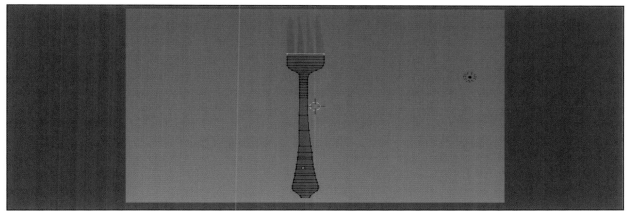

Step 4: This is the tricky part and it has to be done right. More vertices are needed, but figuring a way to add them which won't cause problems is vexing. More will be spoken of this during the discussion. The best way to get the desired vertices is by adding additional edges with CNTR + R. However, the first part of the shaft needs to be temporarily deleted. Select the vertices in the picture.

Note: Yours should be reasonably similar.

Selected   Deleted

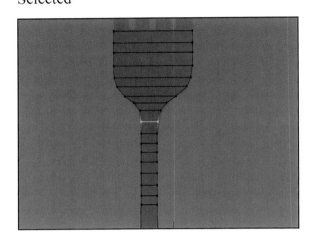
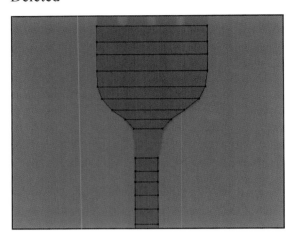

Step 5: Ok, 6 Edges (CNTR + R) will be added. Add them vertically, one at a time and move them into place, -to the corresponding fork prongs. Reference the pictures.

CNTR + R (left click and position)   Add the second one in the same manner

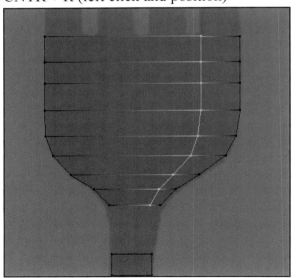
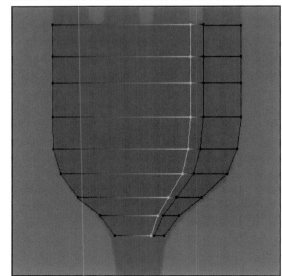

Continue on until this is reached (see next picture).

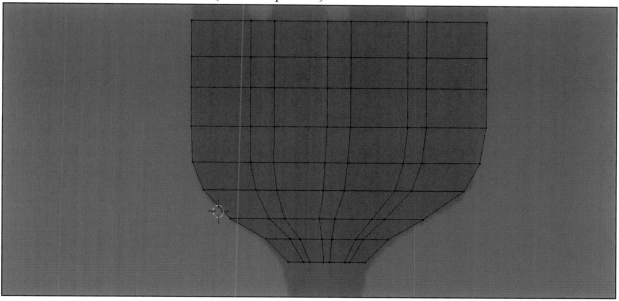

Step 6: Now it is time to merge the vertices at the bottom, -follow along:

Select, then W → Merge at center

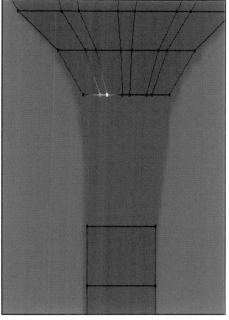

Merged

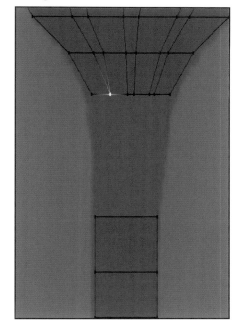

Do the same for the two others to the right, one by one.

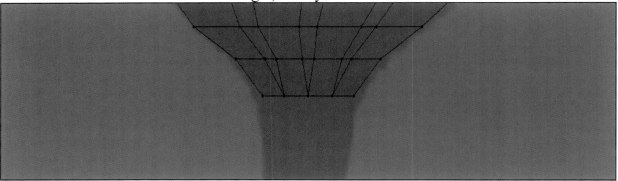

Now select them and Hit E to extrude.

Selected

Hit E, extrude down

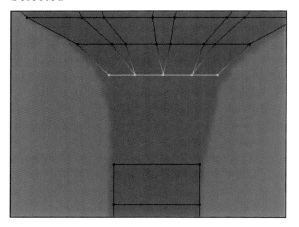
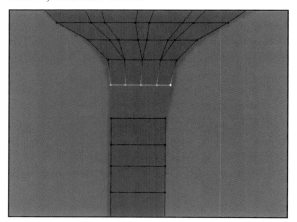

Select the 3 middle vertices of the last extrusion and merge (W key) them at center.

Selected

W key, merge at center

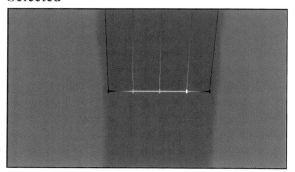

Reference Images

The last part consists of knitting it all together with 3 triangles.

Selected

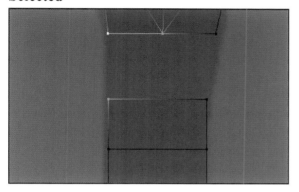

F to fill

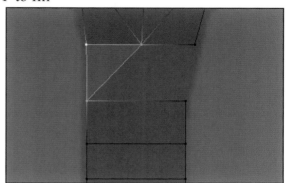

Selected

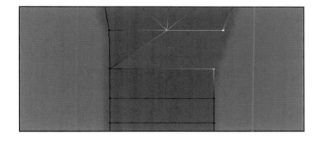

F to fill

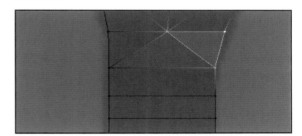

And finally the last center triangle.

Selected

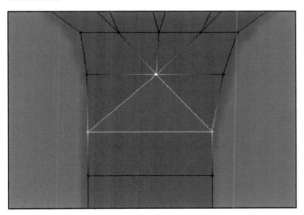

F to fill

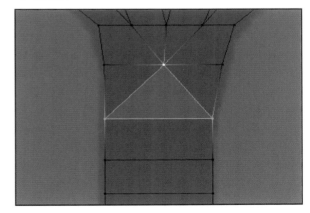

3D Modeling

Step 7: With the neck knitted together, the prongs can now be completed. Start with the one on the left and extrude a couple of times. Scale as you go, and the last two will have to be rotated and grabbed.

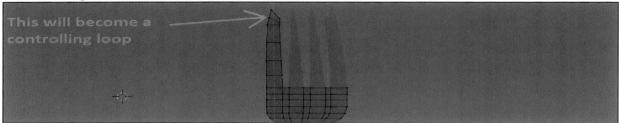

Step 8: Continue on with the rest of the forks. Remember to keep the number of extrusions the same for each prong. Your result should look similar to this.

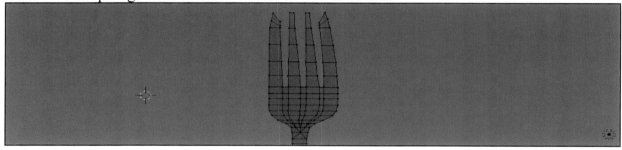

Step 9: Things should be coming together now. Modeling in the bottom scene is now done and it is time to move to the top window with the Right Hand orthographic view. Pull the window down to give yourself some more space. My background image for the side view of the fork is a little bit smaller (the fork) than the one in the lower view. Hit A to select the entire fork, scale and move it until it is the same length as the one in the picture.

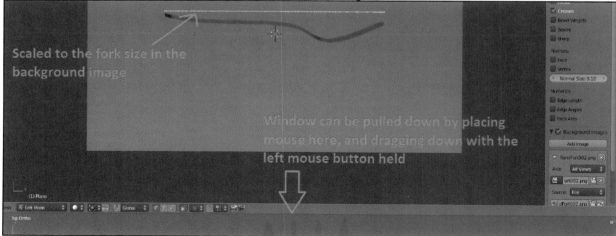

Note: If using B to select the fork to scale, make sure Limit Selection to Visible is Off.

Step 10: The normal occurrence in this situation would be hitting A to deselect the mesh, and then selecting the vertices of each extrusion and moving them into the position of the fork. However, there is a better method. It can be done in one shot with the curve modifier and it will give better results. Now is a perfect time to use the curve. Go to Add → Curve → Path. It will not be visible, hit R to rotate, then Z and then 90 on the numpad. Notice that it popped you into Object Mode. Blender does this automatically when creating curves. Tab back into Edit Mode, and don't be alarmed by the fact that the fork mesh is no longer visible.

Step 11: Scale it up to the size of the fork and subdivide the curve 2 times with the W key. This will give plenty of manipulation points. Move them down (right click on them) one-by-one and trace over the fork.

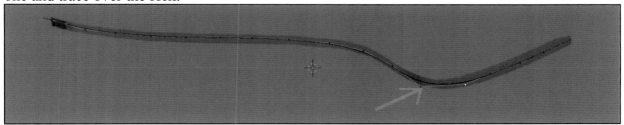

Note: Two lines are present in the curve. The black line is the real curve. The manipulation points riding the orange line are for shaping.

Step 12: Great, the curve is complete and all that needs to be done is to apply it to the fork mesh. This isn't hard, but has to be done correctly. Tab into Object Mode, and select the fork mesh, then hit the Modifiers tab. Select the Curve modifier, and in the Curve pane, select Curve as the Object. See the picture below. Remember, apply the modifier to 'the mesh waiting to be deformed,' then tell the curve modifier what available curve it should follow.

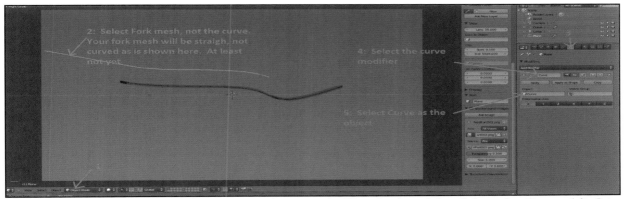

Step 13: Great, but the fork is not properly curved. Here is the trick. Select the Curve, hit G to grab it and place it over top of the fork mesh. It will perfectly deform it to the curve shape.

Note: You may have to tilt the view to see everything a little clearer. This is what you should have.

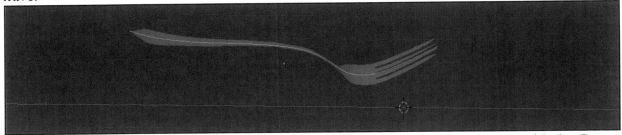

It is a beautiful fork. In the Curve Modifier panel, hit Apply. You are now done with the Curve, select it, hit X and delete it.

Step 14: This is the homestretch. Select the fork mesh and tab into Edit Mode. Now is a good time to save. **File → Save → Fork002.**

Let's give the fork some depth. Tap the A key to select the entire fork mesh and hit E to extrude. Pull down and give it some depth. It would be better to overestimate the thickness, as people have a tendency to make them too thin.

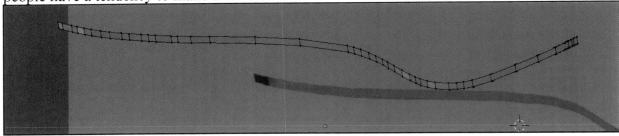

Step 15: Fantastic, select the fork and go to the Modifiers tab. Select a Subdivision Surface modifier. Set the **View** and **Render** levels to 2. Position the camera to your view (CNTRL + ALT + 0) and hit F12 for a render.

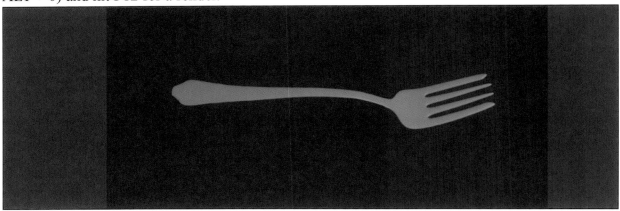

Note: Very little was done to this rendered image. Ambient Occlusion was set to .2 and the background color was set to Blend. That is it.

Discussion:

This exercise was the longest to date, but worth it. If finishing it successfully, or at least reasonably well, there should have been wow effect; as in, wow, I can really model. This fork could easily make its way into any animated movie, still shot, or video game.

The fork was selected for a number of reasons. First of all, it was not all that complicated in terms of background image usage. While most models use 3 or more images (FRONT, TOP, SIDE), the fork only required 2. In addition, resizing the images and lining them up was not required for this tutorial. It was your author's expressed desire to show some mercy in this regard and allow new students to painlessly experiment with this technique.

This fork tutorial was also chosen for another reason. Modeling a fork is incredibly deceptive for newcomers. Take some time to look over some of the pitfalls in modeling this fork incorrectly. What you will see may be an eye opener. Don't go back and model these yourself, just read this section and make a strong mental note of what is occurring with such mistakes and the ramifications.

Mistake #1 Would be made by newbies when initially trying to do this for themselves.
When figuring out a way to add extra vertices, most beginners would just subdivide the last extrusion as such.

Then they would use the new vertices to make the prongs, and hey, there are some extra ones to massage into the rounded areas between the prongs. Great huh? Not really, when finished and with the Subdivision Surface modifier applied, this is what happens.

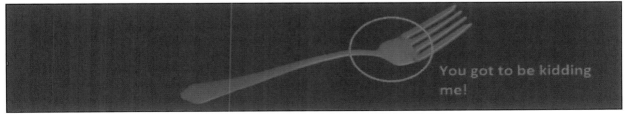

Fixing this would require adding some controlling loops and messing around with the topology. Unfortunately, this is a messy proposition, requiring a little too much work.

Mistake #2 Would be made by a slightly more experienced newbie.

Any beginner looking at mistake #1, that had enough experience would see that 'having all new triangles' from the subdivisions (W) will cause problems when smoothed (modifier). A clever person would temporarily delete the second to last extrusion, then subdivide the line, and then reconnect it with fill. This avoids all those nasty triangles. Follow along with the pictures.

Second to last extrusion deleted

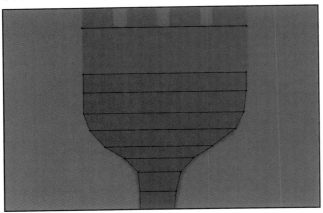

Last extrusion subdivided multiple times

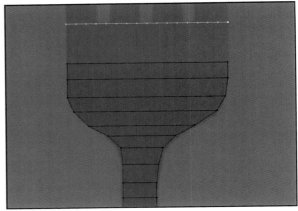

Select the 4 points

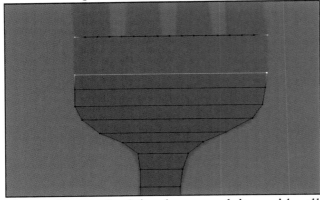

Filled with the F key

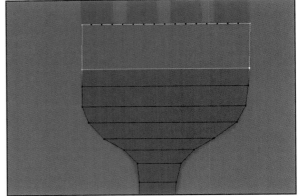

Great, this method is clever, and it avoids all those nasty triangles. The vertices are not anchored down (connected), but if the modeler is careful, it should not matter. Using this technique works perfectly right up until the Subdivision Surface modifier is applied. When finished, this is what happens.

What a mess, that little trick of having non-anchored vertices came with a price. See how it creases right along the vertices which are non-anchored and also pinches in the sides. So much for being clever.

Mistake #3 A beginner understanding the problems with mistakes 1 and 2, might eventually understand that adding additional edges to get the needed vertices for the prongs is the way to go. However, they may not understand the problem with the fork tapering down at the stem. If the new edges are not disconnected from the stem, then a whole lot of unnecessary vertices would be created. See picture below.

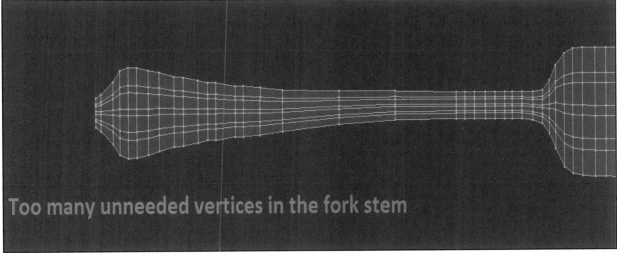

Too many unneeded vertices in the fork stem

This is bad, but it isn't the worst situation in the world. The real problem begins when the

Subdivision Surface modifier is applied at level 3.

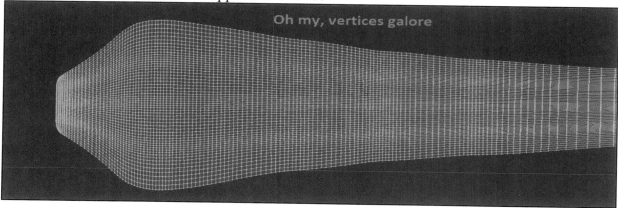

Even quad-core systems wouldn't like munching down this many vertices. As can be seen, having the newly added edges come down into the stem would have been a major mistake. Keep these mistakes in mind when doing future modeling. Good topology is good for a reason.

Chapter 12: Colorization

Exercise # 1 Adding Color to a Mesh

Step 1: Start a new scene, keep the cube and go to the material Tab on the right. Click the New button. Under Diffuse, click on the white colored selection box, and move the dot to the desired location on the color wheel. Choose a nice blue. To the right of the color wheel is a vertical scroll column. This increases or decreases the saturation. Play with it! Hit F12 and render. Simple as pie!

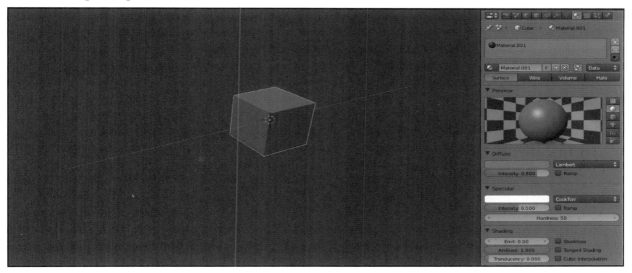

3D Modeling

Exercise # 2 Adding Multiple Colors to a Mesh

Step 1: Adding multiple colors to one mesh is also simple. Start with a new scene, delete the Cube with X. Add a UV Sphere: Add → Mesh → UV sphere. Go to the Material tab, click the New button, and select a color under Diffuse. Go for a dark blue.

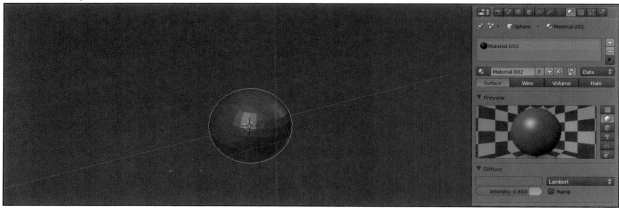

Step 2: To add the second color, vertices (or faces) must be selected. Be sure to tab into Edit Mode. Once in Edit Mode, deselect the entire mesh by hitting A. Hit 1 one the numpad. Turn Limit Selection to Visible **Off,** and select the entire middle section with the B key.

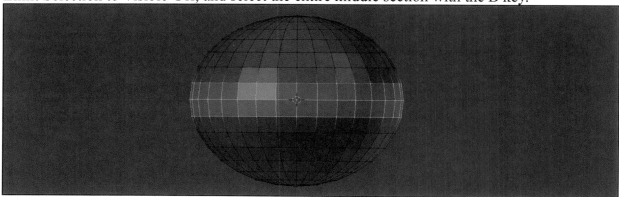

Step 3: Hit the plus on the top. *Note: **Be careful here, don't choose the one below.***

Colorization

Then hit the New button.

Under Diffuse, select a mustard yellow color (or something close), and click Assign.

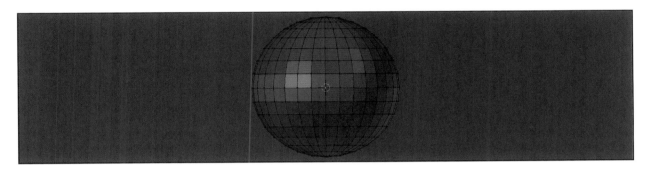

Step 4: Add a Subdivision Surface modifier and set the **View** and **Render** levels to 4. Tab into Object Mode, duplicate existing lamp (SHFT + D) and position them. Then position the camera to your view. Hit F12 and render the scene.

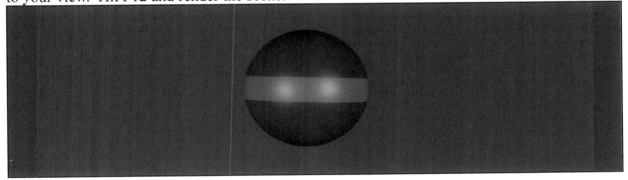

A perfect croquet ball!

Chapter 13: Textures

Adding textures is the next big step in creating more realistic models. They are not always necessary, as the croquet ball demonstrated. However, they help out a great deal at eliminating that ultra-smooth, plastic-like appearance, which dominated early 3D cartoons. Models should only look ultra smooth and glossy when it is called for. Everything else typically demands textures. The unfortunate reality of textures is their complexity. This is one area of modeling that is rough, and it's not a GUI problem; some things are just complex by nature. Texturing is an exceedingly large topic to say the least.

The simplest way for a beginner to handle textures is to use a photo (self taken or legal web resource) and add a secondary inbuilt texture which only utilizes normal values (gives a raised look). While not a procedural panacea, this two shot approach gets the job done more often than not. By simply using a real photo, much of the work associated with getting the settings correct is eliminated. Certain metrics will still need adjustment, such as reflection, lighting, gloss, light scattering, and so-on. Fear not, as this is little more than knob turning.

Note: The process of using camera photos as textures will be taught in the peanut butter cup tutorial at the end of the book. This chapter will deal with more general aspects of texturing.

Exercise # 1 Using Default Textures (Speckled Gumball)
Let's say you have to create a gumball machine, and that is done, but the gumballs have yet to be completed. This is the task at hand. Using nothing more than a colored sphere is fine, but adding a texture will create a more professional look.
Step 1: Start with a new scene, and delete the cube. Add → Mesh → UV Sphere. Click the Smooth Shading button on the left (while still in Object Mode).
Step 2: Select the Material tab and click the color box under Diffuse. Select a nice purple.

Textures

Note: Always first add a material to a mesh when adding textures. The settings can be left blank for those not wanting an initial color (i.e., those typically using photos).

Step 3: Go to the Texture button (scroll to it using the MMB) and click New. Go to Type, and select NOISE from the menu.

Step 4: To smooth it out a little more, add a Subdivision Surface Modifier at level 2 for both the **View** and **Render** levels.

Step 5: Hit F12.

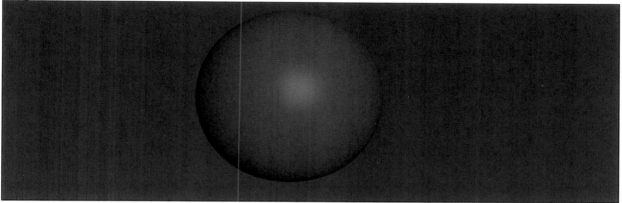

Note: It looks much better than just a standard gumball, and very little work was done to obtain it.

The pink color which is showing through can be changed. The setting for doing so is at the bottom of the texture pain. Change it to whatever is desired. A light yellow was chosen here. Hit F12 again.

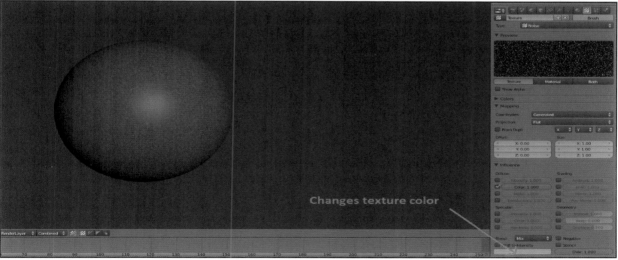

In the interest of saving time, this exercise will be used for the next tutorial. Save it as **Gumball001**.

Exercise # 2 Raised Textures with Normal Values

Some textures are saved with normal values included. This allows for a little trick to be done by way of the normal value setting when texturing. The textures can actually have perceived height, which removes the dreaded flat look.

Note: Not all textures have normal values baked in.

Step 1: Make sure the Gumball001.blend file is open and you are at the Materials tab. Same as the previous picture.

Step 2: In the texture pane, go down to where it says **Influence**. Under Geometry, put a check beside **Normal**.

Step 3: F12.

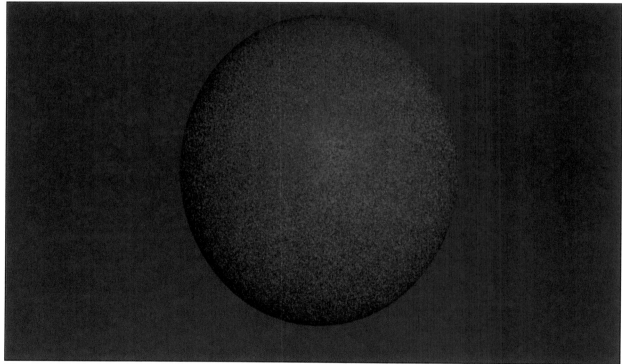

The gumball now has a raised texture, but it looks horrid, -almost as if a strange disease has taken hold. We want a raised texture on this, but something which looks good. As this is hideous, remove the check mark beside the normal value. Luckily, we can add multiple textures to one object. In this case, we are going to add an additional texture to the gumball which makes it bumpy, but does nothing else.

Step 4: Follow the picture below for adding an additional texture to the gumball. This additional texture will only use the normal values.

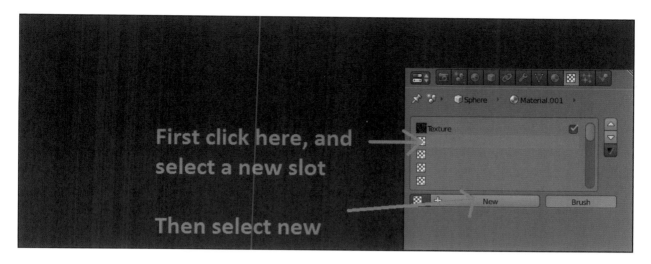

In the next picture only, follow the instructions from bottom to top (the order is reversed here).

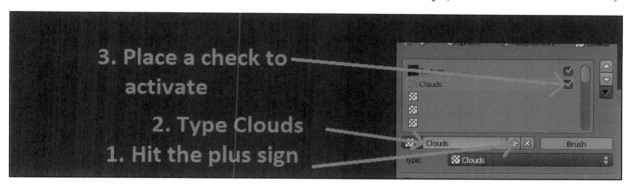

Great, the clouds texture is selected by default, and luckily enough, that is what we are using.

Step 5: All that has to be done now is to place a check beside Normal under Geometry. And one other thing, uncheck the Color.
Note: An additional color with this texture is unneeded, and unwanted.

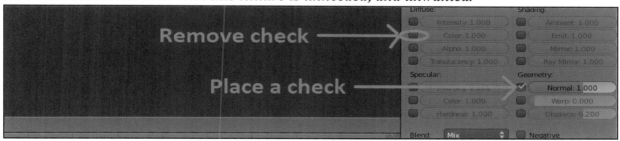

Step 6: F12, the results are shown on the next image.

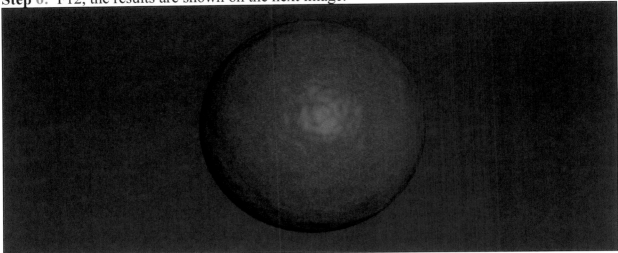

Again, very cool and completed with little effort. You're a beginner and just made a speckled gumball with a bumpy texture that even the best professional modelers couldn't trump! As with the fork exercise, a sense of accomplishment should be taking hold. The power of Blender should be apparent at this point.

If spare time is at hand, play around with different coloration. Have fun and do whatever is desired.

Discussion: What is being seen here with the raised normal values adding bumpiness is nothing more than a complete illusion. Even though the gumball looks bumpy, there are no real bumps there; it is nothing more than a smoke n' mirror shading trick; albeit one done very well! This technique is great because it does not add extra vertices to calculate, but it does have one downfall. When this texture is applied to a plain, when looking straight at it, everything looks fine.

However, if it is tilted down to almost being horizontal, the raised effect vanished.

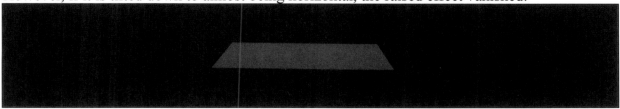

This is an inherent weakness of using normal values to raise textures! It only works straight on, and the lower you get on the horizon, the greater the diminishing of the effect. Is there a way to add this bumpy cloud texture and have it display at this angle? The next exercise demonstrates this.

Exercise # 3 Raised Textures with the Displace Modifier

Unlike using normal values to simulate raised textures, the Displace modifier actually pushes the vertices up. This does however come with a price. More vertices (dramatically more) need to be used in the base mesh. As should be mentioned, the displace modifier is not a true texture, it is a mesh modification. However, it can create effects comparable to normal values, and is presented here for that reason.

Step 1: Start with a new scene. Delete the cube with X, and Add → Mesh → Plane. Tab into Edit Mode and subdivide the plane 7 times. As stated, extra vertices are needed for proper displacement.

Step 2: Tab back into Object Mode, go to the Materials tab and add a new material. Add a nice purple color as before.

Step 3: Go to the texture tab and add a new texture. Select noise and set the color (at the bottom, to yellow); this will give the yellow speckles as before with the gumball. A quick way to check that everything is alright is to quickly click in the Material tab and take a look at the preview. As can be seen in the picture below. The preview is purple with yellow speckles.

Step 4: Great, go back to the Texture Tab and add another texture.

Then click New and select Clouds (as before). Name the Texture Clouds, and uncheck the box to the right. This (unchecking) basically says that you don't want to apply the texture to this material, but it is available for use with other things, such as the Displace Modifier.

Step 5: Almost done, go to the Modifier Tab and select a new Displace Modifier.

Caution: Don't confuse this with the Mesh Deform modifier, only select Displace. Tab into Object Mode (the effect will only be visible in Object Mode).

In the Displace Modifier panel, select Clouds as the texture (it should have been named that) and set .100 as the strength.

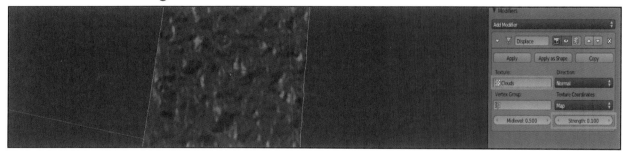

Click Apply to finalize the Displace modifier. The following low angled picture shows the bumps from the displacement are really there, and not faked.

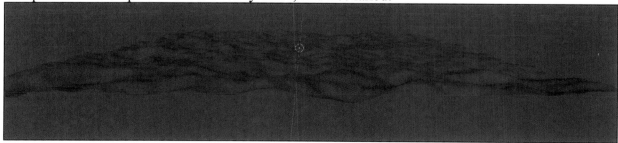

The Displace Modifier is reminiscent of a stamping machine.

Discussion:

A lot more can be done with this mesh. Another Displace modifier could be added. If desired, take some time with adding multiple Displace modifiers. Sometimes it is not about making drastic changes, but perhaps adding the same one again, and slightly changed the texture size to increase randomness.

The displace modifier can also accept black n' white images (loaded as a texture) and project the black area as a texture. To do this, render any mesh with a white background (in world settings) and no lights. Use a screen-shot tool (such as greenshot) and save it as a JPEG or PNG image. ***Note: Saving a rendered image can also be done in Blender by hitting F3 (this method is preferable for serious renders).*** The load it as a texture. Only the outline will be seen.

Users can also use their own rendered textures with normal values. As an example, the monkey could be used to create an 'alien coming through the skin' effect. This process is done though baking tangent normal maps. It is the same as rendering, with the addition of normal values being baked in. This process, while not difficult, will not be demonstrated here.

Exercise # 4 Raised Textures with Sculpt Mode (Claymation Bark Texture)
Step 1: Start with a new scene, delete the cube. Add → Mesh → Plane. Hit 7 and 1 on the numpad, then tab into Edit Mode. Subdivide the cube 6 times with the W key.
Step 2: Down where it says "Edit Mode," switch it to Sculpt Mode. In the left hand pane, select Clay (click on the picture to change it) as the brush. Set the Strength to ~.8 and click on Subtract.
Step 3: Make the cube fairly large on the screen (using the Middle Mouse Button) and make a series of north to south strokes holding the down the middle mouse button. The idea is to start making them look as though they are bark. Make them random to some extent.

Blah, it's an ugly, blurry, pixel-crazed mess. No worries, it is just oversized right now. Yours will undoubtedly look different, but yet similar.

Step 4: Good, almost done now. Switch to Object Mode, click Smooth in the right hand panel. Go to Material, and set the color as a nice brown. In the material pane, turn the Specular Intensity down to .093 (bark is not that reflective).

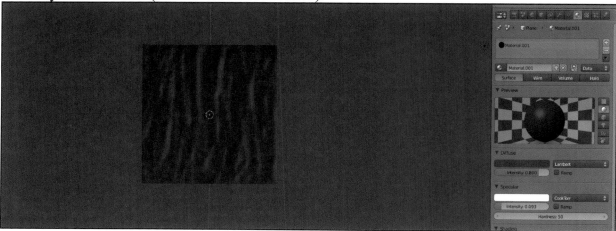

Step 5: F12 if desired.

Note: Technically speaking, this is not actually a texture, it is mesh manipulation by way of the sculpt tool. Any which way you slice it, the end result looks like a texture, and it is presented as such. The same is true for the Displace modifier.

Chapter 14: UV Mapping

UV Mapping is another form of texturing. The first question to ask is why anyone would use this method of texturing over the standard method. The common answer is that it works well for curved surfaces, and this is especially true when using images. With regard to curved surfaces, it allows for greater mapping control in an effort to reduce distortion. That being said, UV mapping can be used on flat surfaces. The rule of thumb is to use it when general texturing does not seem to suffice. Understanding when and where it should be used will come naturally after a while.

Exercise # 1 UV Texturing a Small Box
Step 1: Pick a box, a small box, nothing fancy here. It could be a box of band-aids, eye drops, or butter. The idea here is to pick anything small, and rectangular.
Cut the box open EXACTLY as the template shows.

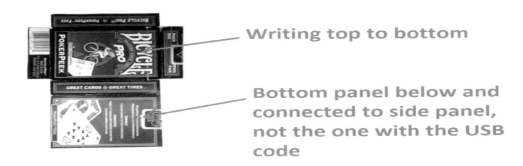

Writing top to bottom

Bottom panel below and connected to side panel, not the one with the USB code

3D Modeling

As a reminder, most commercial packaging boxes have a thin layer of lacquer, which is highly reflective. Diffused lighting is best in such situations. As can be seen in the previous photo, the bottom panel is reflecting too much light.

Step 2: Fire up Blender and start a new scene. Use the default cube and tab into Edit Mode. Here is your job. Scale the box on any needed axes until it roughly takes shape of your box. It does not have to be perfect in terms of dimension, and a background picture is not needed. Just get it close. Once you have the box virtually replicated, click Edge Select and mark the same edges as seen in the bottom picture. I have switched to wireframe mode to eliminate the occlusion of background geometry. Doing the same on your end is not required.

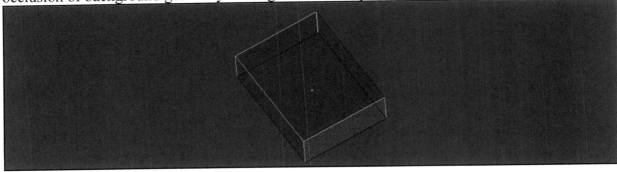

This is going to be the unwrapping seam.

Step 3: In the tool shelf on the left, go down to where it says UV Mapping and click the Mark Seam button. Tap the A key, and the seam should turn red.

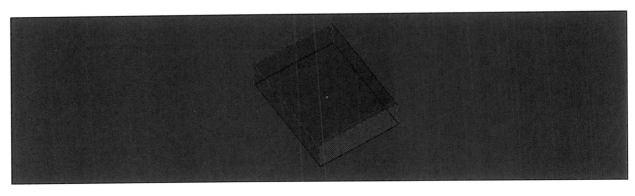

Step 4: Great, now the window needs to be split. You remember how to do that, right. Well, if not, go down to the very bottom left of the 3d view port and place the mouse cursor over the tiny cobwebs in the corner. A plus sign should appear, and when it does drag it over to the right. Right next to the cobwebs (left caddy-corner) is where the window type can be changed. Click on it and select UV/Image Editor.

UV Mapping

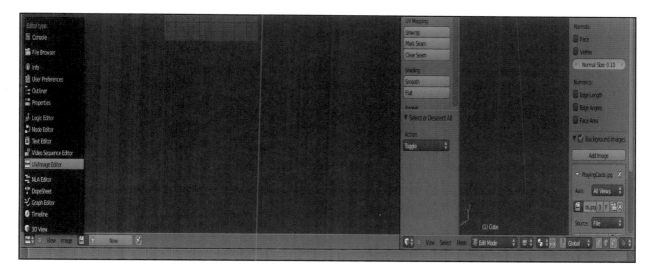

Step 5: This is the easy part, place your mouse cursor anywhere in the right hand viewport. Make sure you are in EDIT MODE, and hit A to select the entire box. Hit the U key and unwrap. Great, it unwrapped properly into the crucifix shape. Don't worry if yours is positioned differently (on its side).

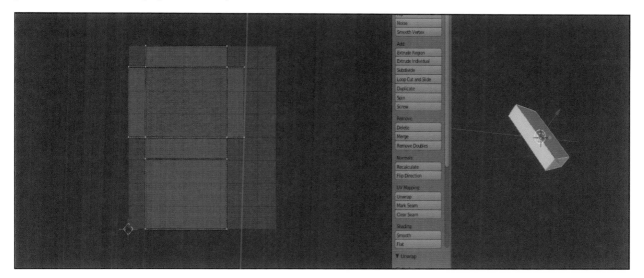

Step 6: The picture of your box now needs to be loaded. Keep your mouse in the UV/Mapping viewport, and hit ALT + o (stands for open) and load your image.
Note: Blender does not accept all files types. PNG is always a safe bet. Use a program such as GIMP and re-save the image as PNG if needed.

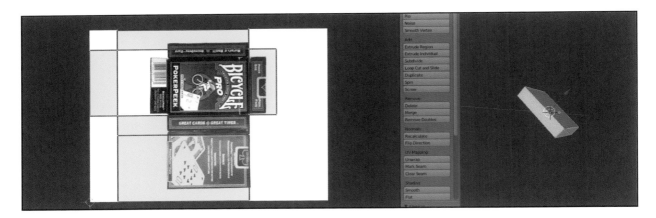

Step 7: Great, now all that has to be done is to line everything up. The unwrapped mesh can be manipulated just as any other mesh. *Note: **If yours unwrapped sideways, just hit R and rotate it 90 degrees.*** The example above is fine. Once that is done, hit A to deselect the vertices and move each one individually into position. The below picture shows the current alignment. It is a simple overlay.

Step 8: Now the fun part, in the right window with the original mesh, select Textured as the Viewport Shading (beside where is says Edit Mode)

UV Mapping

Fabulous, hit F12 and do a render with a little Environment lighting added.

Blah, it didn't render. Blender needs a little more information. Go to the Material tab and add a new material. Don't do anything with it, but immediate click on the Texture button and add a new texture.

While in the Texture panel:
1. For Type, select Image or Movie and load the image.
2. Go down to Image and click Open. Load the box image.
3. Go down to Mapping (NOT Image Mapping, just Mapping) and set the coordinates to UV.

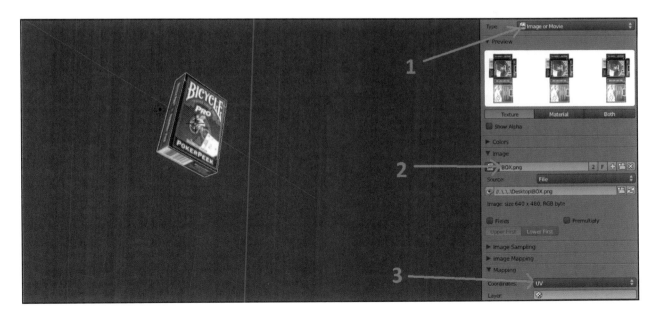

Step 9: Set up the lighting any which way, mine has a little Environment lighting (.25), and do a render.

Discussion:

That was a lot of work for a simple image texture, now wasn't it. Not to mention, the process was not exactly intuitive. However, some positives must be noted. When the box was modeled, it was not a perfect match to what the real "cut-out" box was in terms of dimension. UV mapping allows you to fudge things a little without there being a problem. And that is the purpose of this exercise, -to show how UV Mapping allows for alignment of maps (images) onto meshes that may not be in perfect dimension.

That being said, UV mapping has a ton of problems. The first of which is how to properly mark the seams to get it to unwrap in the desired manner. As for our exercise, had the physical box been cut wrong, it would not have projected in the correct direction. Here is an example of what would have occurred if the back panel was left connected to the bottom panel with the USB strip (which actually seems more natural).

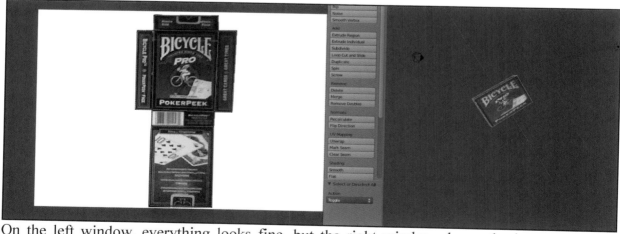

On the left window, everything looks fine, but the right window shows the image mapping sideways! This is frustrating for beginners.

UV Mapping

   Additional problems with UV mapping include stretching issues, seams (which have to be hidden), along with a bunch of other nuances. Going over these and how to fix them could be done, but it would be better for beginners to move on at this point.

Chapter 15: Lighting

Up until this point, very little has been given with regard to lighting instruction. While seemingly simple, lighting is a very complex subject matter, and one which beginners will need to spend a great deal of time experimenting with. Making very subtle changes in light distance, strength, properties, and attributes makes for profound changes in the visual representation. The problem at hand is not with understanding how any given lighting system works, but the endless combinations of different systems being used to create an effect. The goal here is to make lighting exceedingly simple for the new user and in doing so, the exercises will be presented in reverse order. Automated lighting will be shown first, and then manual setups. The monkey will be used as the test subject for all exercises.

Exercise # 1 Ambient Occlusion

Ambient Occlusion (AO) is a lighting method designed to create realism with non-direct light. In other words, the type of lighting seen on an overcast day. This is the general layperson's explanation, but it speaks poorly with regard to the end-state visuals. This is your authors personal explanation of Ambient Occlusion: "AO is a highly automated lighting method, which creates a stuck-on light effect, while maintaining shading (darker areas)." At times, it will be used as 100% of the lighting, completely omitted, or used sparingly and mixed with other lighting methods. It is all a matter of what is called for. With that said, AO is very easy to implement.

Lighting

Step 1:   Start a new scene, delete the cube with X, and add the monkey (Add → Mesh → Monkey). Hit 5 and 7 on the numpad.

Step 2:   Hit Smooth while in Object Mode and add a Subdivision Surface modifier, with the **View** and **Render** levels set to 3. This will make for a nice smooth monkey.

Note: This same setup will be used for the next 2 exercises.

Step 3:   Select the default point light and hit X to delete it.

Step 4:   Time for some fun. Go to the World Tab (Planet Icon) on the right, and in the panel, put a check beside Ambient Occlusion. Place the camera to your view with CNTRL + ALT + 0. Hit F12 and render.

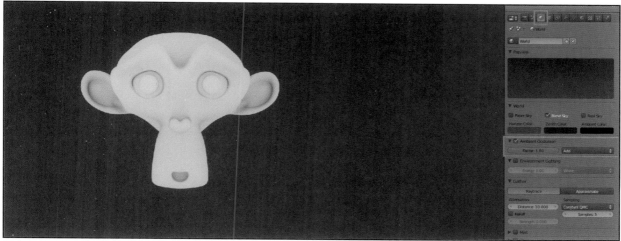

It is way too bright, but look at the ears, notice how AO preserves darker shading.

Step 5:   Under the Ambient Occlusion check box, turn the factor down to .5 and do another render.

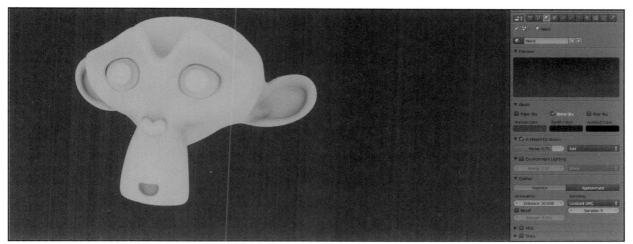

Ahhh, much better. AO can be used in conjunction with other lighting methods. It is typical for a little AO to be used with normal lighting. Examples will not be given, as that can be experimented with in your own time.

Note: If moving onto the next exercise immediately, keep the current scene, but uncheck the box for Ambient Occlusion.

Exercise # 2 Environment Lighting

Ambient Occlusion has a cousin known as Environment lighting. It is basically a cheap way to mimic global illumination. Global illumination can be though of as having the mesh surrounded by an icosphere, which has a light on every vertex. In other words, light coming at the mesh from from all directions. This was how Environment lighting was done in previous versions of Blender, it was a manually setup. It is good for outdoor scenes.

Step 1: Click the Environment lighting check-box and render the scene with F12.

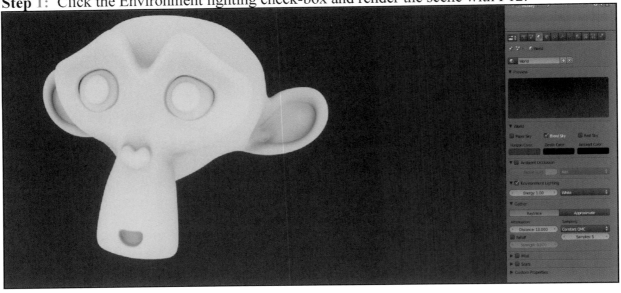

Notice how much Environment lighting looks like AO in this shot. Environment lighting supposedly does not have the same stuck-on light effect, but one can't argue, the end product is nearly identical to that of AO in this circumstance. This is true, even when coloration and textures are added. However, differences will be seen in other setups.

Exercise # 3 Three Point Lighting

When it comes to lighting, it's never long before 3 point lighting is mentioned. Its use goes all the way back to early film and has become a standard of sorts. Before moving on to the exercise, let's take a minute to go over some of the main concepts of this lighting system.

Lighting

Three point light starts with a key light. This is the main light which has the highest strength. It is usually a warm color such as light yellow or light orange. This gives a more natural lighting effect (sunlight). With most 3 point lighting, spot lights are used. If the light is selected, the lamp tab can be clicked on, which has all the changeable attributes of the light. In this case, the size was reduce, the color changed, the strength increased to 1.5, and the default of having shadows was maintained. It is typically positioned to the right caddy-corner. This is how most people set up the key light.

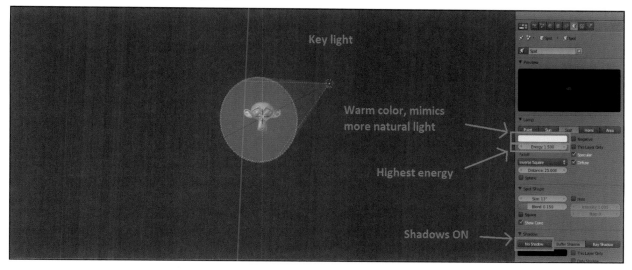

Then a fill light is added. This is also a spot light. It is placed off the the left, and a little lower than the key light. It is set at a lower energy level, and generally colored a light blue. Its job is to knock out the shadows created by the key light, and create a cooling effect.

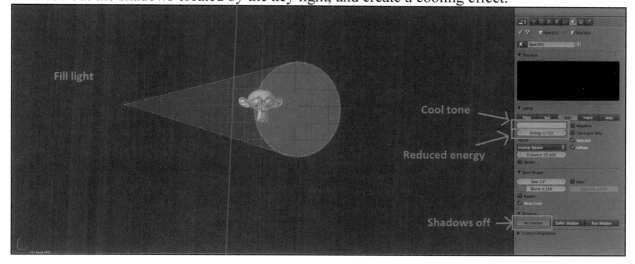

Last, but not least is the back-light. It's job is to create and enhanced outline of the mesh.

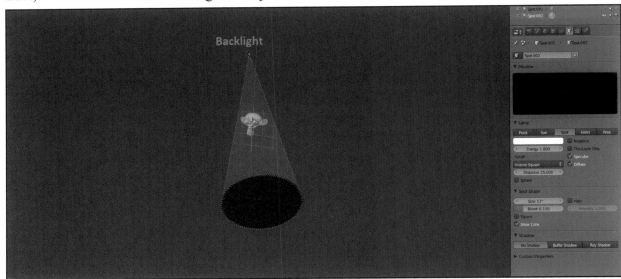

However, the spotlight in this position does not seem to do all that much. Apparently, certain aspects of film stage setups do not exactly mirror that of 3D modeling. Many modelers have dumped this spotlight in favor of a Hemi lamp. The Hemi lamp sits in the same place as the backlight normally would, but the Hemi wraps light around the front of the mesh to a greater degree. The Hemi location is typically in the back and a little off to the left. The final setup with the Hemi lamp will look as such.

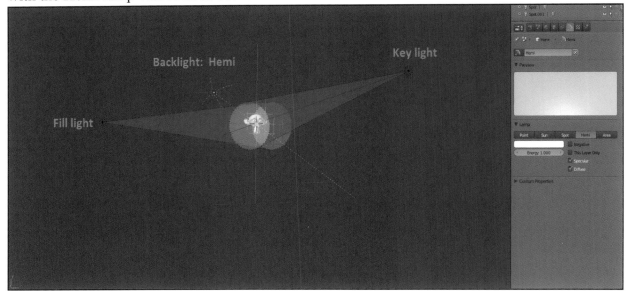

Lighting

Ok, great, that is it, right? Not exactly, this lighting setup is a pain to position, and a lot of time goes into getting the distances right, not to mention the correct energy levels. Yes, it is the industry standard, but truth be told, it is not even a real 3 point lighting setup. The backlight is now a Hemi and even though it is in back of the monkey, it wraps light around the front of it. That is not what a traditional back-light is supposed to do. Traditional back-lights are for increasing outlines. This is especially true of dark objects on dark backgrounds. It stops the camouflaging.

For beginners starting out with throw-away models, this is not necessary. A hassle-free, simple lighting setup should be utilized. Be forewarned, this will anger many people who have been relying on time consuming spotlights n' Hemi setups.

Step 1: Keep the monkey setup, and keep the default point light as the key light. If it was deleted, a new one needs to be added. After adding it, hit SHFT + D and duplicate it. Use one as the Key and one as the fill. Position them as such and enter the shown values in the following picture. Lastly, Go to the world tab, put a check beside Environment Lighting and enter .20 as the Energy.

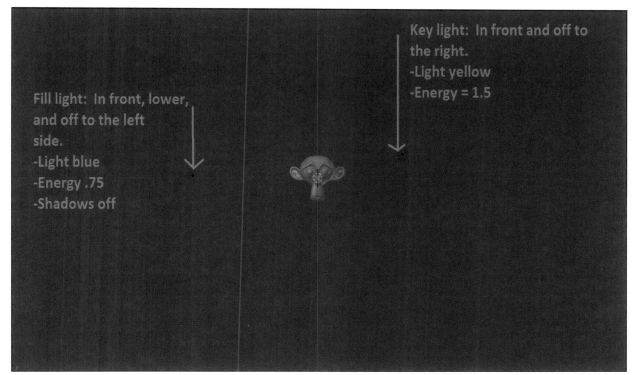

Step 2: That is all there is to it. Position the camera to the desired view with CNTRL + ALT + 0 and hit F12.

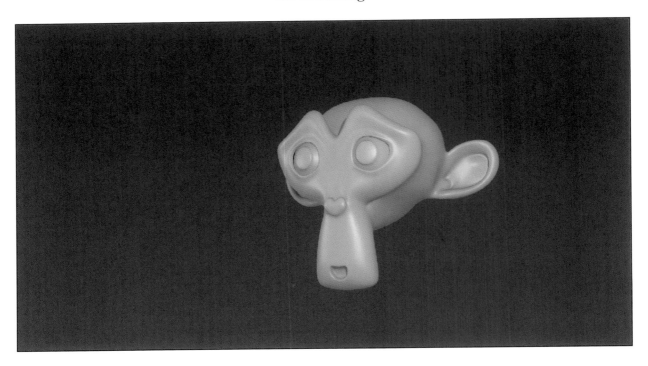

It is an extremely good result considering the simplicity of this lighting setup. The reflections actually look good on this model, but what if they are not desired? This is easy enough to control by way of materials.

Step 3: Go to the Material icon, add a new material, but don't change the color. Set .1 as the specular value and render again. As seen below, reflections are minimized.

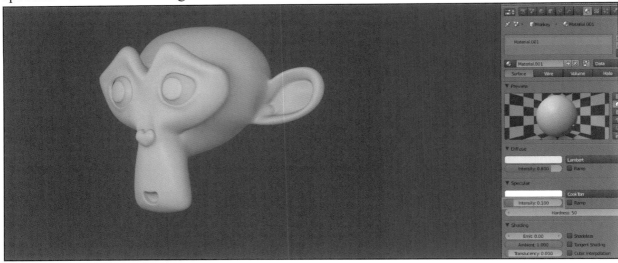

Lighting

Exercise # 4 Indirect Lighting (the Glow Stick)

Indirect lighting is a relatively new feature for Blender. Essentially, Indirect lighting makes objects glow in a uniform manner. Anything can be done from glow in the dark stickers, magical orbs, luminescent fish, or anything else the mind can conjure up. Time for a glow-stick.

Step 1: Start with a new scene, stay in Object Mode, delete the cube, and add a Cylinder (Add → Mesh → Tube).
Step 2: Hit 5 and 1 on the numpad. Hit R to rotate → 90 on the numpad, then left click to finalize the rotation.
Step 3: Hit S to scale, Z to constrain the axis, and scale into a cylinder shape.

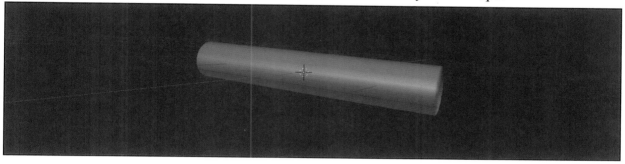

Step 4: The Indirect lighting setup is as follows. Click the world icon on the right → click the check box beside Environment Lighting → Turn the Factor setting up to 1.00. Under Gather, click on Approximate, and put a check beside Falloff.
Step 5: With the cylinder selected, click the Material button. In the Material settings, click New to add a new material. Under DIFFUSE, click the white color box → set the color wheel to a nice luminescent green.
Step 6: In the Material settings, go down to Emit, and set it to 2.5. This setting makes the magic happen. Set up the camera to your view (CNTRL + ALT + 0). Before doing a final render, we want to make sure that the Indirect lighting is actually working. Select the default lamp in the scene, delete it, and hit F12. If it is working, you will see the glow-stick, otherwise, it will be blacked-out.

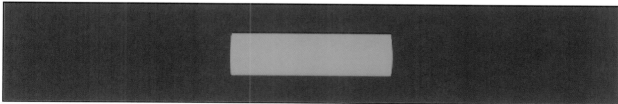

Step 7: Great, it looks descent, but it isn't exactly giving off the expected glow effect. To see this better, add a cube to the seen, tab into Edit Mode, select face mode, and delete one face

with X. Scale up the cube and place it so that the glow-stick is in it. Do another render.

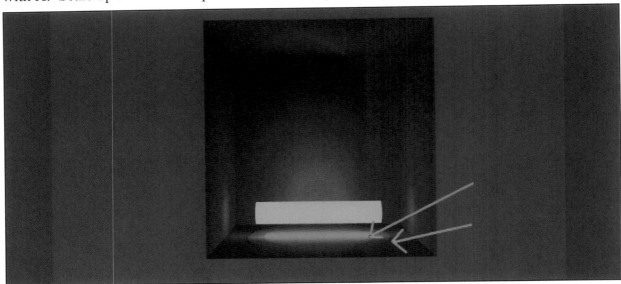

Great, that is the desired effect, but what are those strange rings underneath? No worries, this can be fixed. Go back to the world settings, and under Gather, set the Error value to 0. Render again.

A perfect glow-stick, or perhaps a cute radioactive rod that a certain Springfield employee misplaced.

Note: Indirect lighting is fun! A lot can be done with. When desired, take some time to make different objects and play with the values.

Lighting

Exercise # 5 Subsurface Scattering (Gummy Monkey)

Subsurface Scattering (SSS) is the process by which light enters a semi-translucent object, and is then reflected back at differing angles. Many objects in a real world are semi-translucent. Skin is! Rocks such as marble and garnets are. They all allow light to penetrate to a certain degree. Many modelers often can't figure out as to why they can't get certain models to look realistic in certain situations. They try adding colors and textures, but that 'real-world' realism just isn't there. *Sometimes SSS is the solution!* SSS is not only used to mimic the real-life lighting of semi-translucent objects, but can also come in handy for things such as paper and clay. In these two latter examples, SSS creates a softening effect.

For this example, we are going to create the effect of soft, shinny, -almost jelly-like rubber. The monkey will be used for this example.

Step 1: Start with a new scene, delete the cube with X, and add the monkey (Add → Mesh → Monkey). Hit 7 on the numpad.

Step 2: let's smooth everything out. Go to the material tab and add a Subdivision Surface Modifier. Set the **View** and **Render** levels to 3. Additionally, hit Smooth on the left (while in Object Mode).

Step 3: Now set up the lighting, -nothing fancy here. Click on the default lamp, and duplicate it by hitting shift + D. Place one on the left and one on the right. Leave all other settings as 'default' and place them as such.

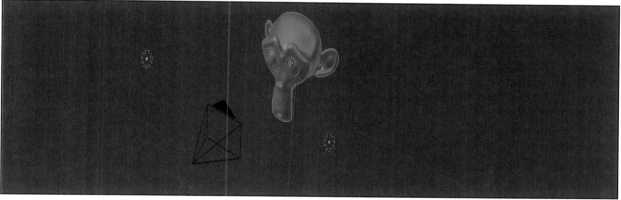

As one final lighting element, click on the World tab and click Ambient Occlusion. Keep the default settings.

Step 4: With the monkey selected (and only the monkey), click on the Material Tab, and select a nice deep red for the Diffuse color. Below Diffuse, put a check beside Subsurface Scattering. Select Ketchup as the preset, and turn the Scatter Color to a light gray. That is it. Hit CNTR + ALT + 0 to position the camera and render the scene. Below is the final rendered image with the Material settings shown.

3D Modeling

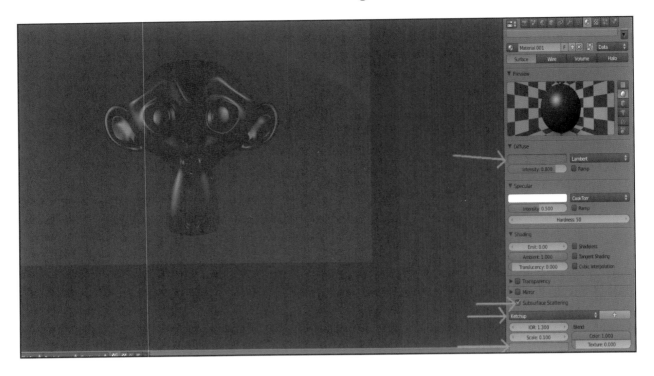

Chapter 16: Models for Beginners

Model 1: Italian Flag (Easy)

Step 1: Start with a new scene, X to delete the cube, add a plane, then 5, and 7 on the numpad. Tab into Edit Mode.

Step 2: Hit W and subdivide the plane 5 times. Then, to keep the number of columns even, add another one to the right via border selecting the edge and hitting E to extrude. Deselect when done.

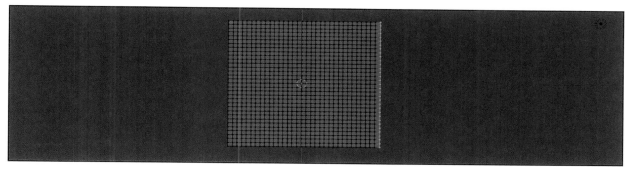

Step 3: Lovely, this will look nice when everything is said and done. Let's add the colors to the flag. We will do all the colors in Edit Mode. Go to the Material tab, click New and add a nice dark Green (under Diffuse). Turn the slider down to increase the saturation.

3D Modeling

Note: Adding the first color is always strange ordeal. First of all, the mesh does not even need to be selected. Second, the first color always covers the entire mesh (it serves as a base coat). Third, the first color does not need to be assigned. Forth, the first color can be added in Object Mode. Strange, strange, strange.

Step 4: Tab into Edit Mode, and while there, Switch to Face Select Mode. Select the middle 11 columns, and hit the plus sign shown in the following picture.

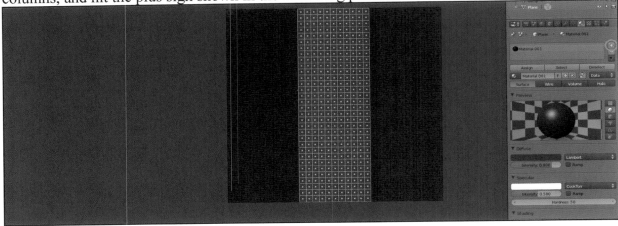

After hitting the plus, a New button should appear. Click it and set (under Diffuse) the new color to nice off white. Remember, the second color must be assigned: Click Assign.
Note: White coloration appears gray in the viewport, but will render correctly.

Step 5: Select the last 11 rows of faces, and click the plus sign again.

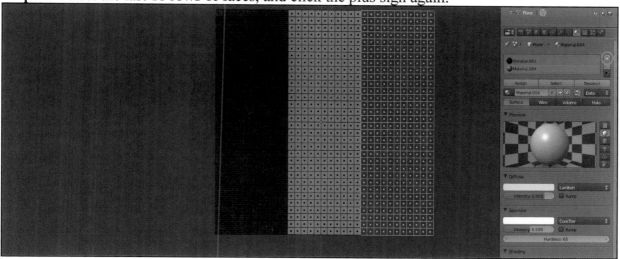

After hitting the plus, a New button will appear again. Click it and set (under Diffuse) the new color to red (perhaps a strong red). Remember, the third color must also be assigned: Click Assign.

Step 9: Here is where the fun begins. Go to the Texture tab, click New → select Marble as the type, and set the Size all the way up to 2. One one last detail, and this is very import; to the right of the Texture slot is a check box, -please uncheck it (ref. next Picture). We do not want the texture to be directly applied to the mesh and unchecking it stops this from happening. What we want is to apply the texture to the Displace modifier. Lastly, name the texture "Marble."

3D Modeling

Step 10: Select the modifiers button, and add a Displace modifier. In the Displace modifier, there is a texture icon under the word Texture, click on it and add the Mable texture that we added. Now turn the Strength down to 0.20.

Step 11: Add a Subdivision Surface modifier, and turn the **View** and **Render** values up to 3. Go to the World button, under Horizon C, change the color to a light blue, and click the check box for Blend. Finally, go the the Render tab, and kick the resolution up to 100%.

Step 12: Position the camera to your view (CNTRL + Alt + 0) and then F12 to render. A nice Italian flag blowing in the wind. See following page for the render.

Discussion:

This exercise was meant to show one thing: Good results can be obtained in Blender without sweating bullets.

Model 2: Peanut Butter Cup (Easy)

Step 1: Start with a new scene, and delete the cube. Add → Mesh → Cylinder. On the left, set the Vertices to 90, and set .3 as the depth. Hit 5 and 1 on the numpad, and tab into Edit Mode.
Step 2: Turn Limit Selection to Visible **Off** and tap A to deselect the entire Cylinder. Using the B key, select only the top vertices of the Cylinder. Hit S and scale them out. Deselect everything with the A key when done.

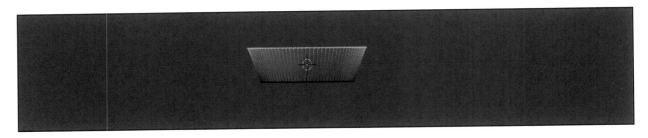

Step 3: Tip the model, and select the very center vertex on the top. Delete it with X.

Step 4: From here we are going to create the same top that was deleted, but with an extra loop to control the downward slop of what will become crimped edges. Select the entire top ridge and hit E to extrude, left click to finalize, and then S to scale.

Selected   E, left click, then S, and move mouse inward

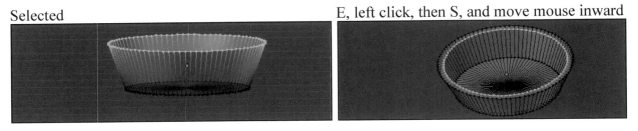

Repeat this procedure one more time. Hit E to extrude, left click to finalize, and then immediately hit S to scale. Bring it all the way into the center, left click, and hit W and merge.

Step 5: Hit 7 on the numpad and select **every other** vertex on the outer rim.

Step 6: With the vertices selected, hit 1 on the numpad, and drag them up with G and scale them out. See the below picture for this.

Note: The crimped ridges are brought up to an unrealistically high level. This is purposeful. The Subdivision Surface modifier will calm these down latter on.

Step 7: Tap the A key to deselect the top vertices. Select all of the vertices between what is now the spikes. Also select the corresponding vertices on on base.

Note: This will take a few minutes. Make sure that all of them are selected and to deselect any vertices which were accidentally selected.

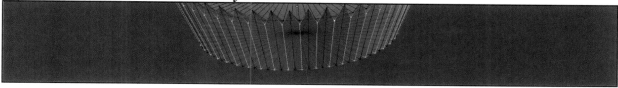

Hit 7 on the numpad, and then S. Scale them in just enough to create those characteristic peanut butter ridges on the side. Not too much. This is an upside down view of what it will look like when done.

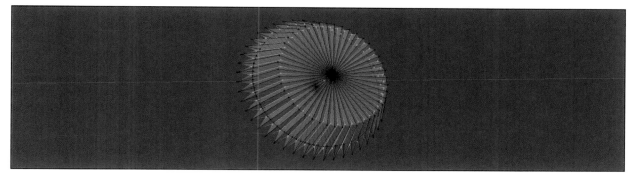

3D Modeling

Step 8: Fantastic, this is coming along swimmingly. Go to the Modifier tab on the right, and add a Subdivision Surface modifier. It really doesn't need to be cranked up much, just set the **View** and **Render** levels to 2.

Step 9: Hit 1 on the numpad and look at the mesh. The Subdivision Surface modifier drastically rounded out the bottom. To rectify this, place the cursor over the mesh, Hit CNTRL + R and add a loop cut. Drag it down to the bottom.

Before loop cut added

After loop cut added

Add another one for the top, just to sharpen the spikes a little. Don't slide it all the way up.

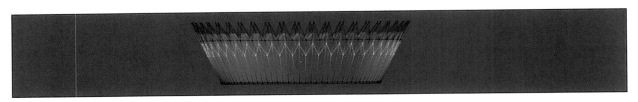

Step 10: The mesh looks good and it is almost time to texture it, but first, a little thinking ahead. It would be nice to have the wrappers on one or both of the peanut butter cups. To create a wrapper, a short cut will be taken via duplicating the existing peanut butter cup and changing it into a wrapper. However, the wrapper should be a new object not linked to the original. To do this, switch to Object Mode, and hit shift + D.

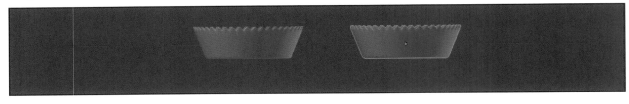

For now, Hit H to hide the duplicate. Let's get back to the original and texture it.

Step 11: With the duplicate hidden, select the original. It's texture time! Go to the Material tab and add a new material, but do nothing else with. To this material, a texture will be added. This is the interesting part.

The best way to go about this is to simply use a close up picture of a peanut butter cup.   This is mine.

For yours, either take a close-up picture yourself, or use a closeup shot from the web (with permission granted). When viewing the picture, use a program such as greenshot to take a cropped screen-shot of the picture. Once the cropped image is saved on your hard drive, go to the Texture tab and add a new texture. To the right of Type, select 'Image or Movie.' Go down to Image, and click on the Open button. Find the chocolate image and click on it, then hit Open. And one final tweak, go all the way to the bottom of the Texture pane and find Image Mapping. Beside Extension, select Extend. This way it does not repeat.

Step 12: Once this is done, do a quick render to see how it looks.

Pretty good, but there is a slight problem. There are ridges (crimping) being created on the top part (flat area). Those are not there on real peanut butter cups! Let's see if that can be rectified. Tab back into Edit Mode, and place a controlling loop using CNTRL + R.

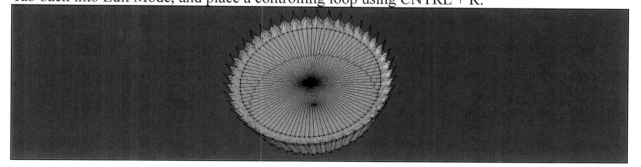

Now here is the trick. With a loop still selected, hit 1 on the numpad, then S to scale, then Z, then 0 on the numpad. In effect, this places all the vertices down flat. Hit Return to finalize the scaling.

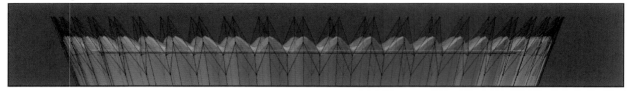

Step 13: Now do another render.

Perfect, those ridges on the top are now gone. The peanut butter cup is now done. Time to work on the wrapper.

Step 14: Unhide the duplicate by hitting ALT + H, then hide the completed peanut butter cup by selecting it and hitting H. Tab into Edit Mode.
Step 15: Select the middle vertex on the top and hit X to delete it.

And continuing on with the deletions, select the inner portion of the crimps, and delete them with X. Warning: This is tricky to do one-by-one. Being in Edge Select Mode and holding Alt and right clicking one of the edges will select the entire loop. Making life easier.

Selected

Deleted

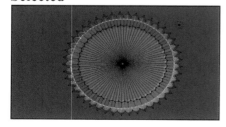
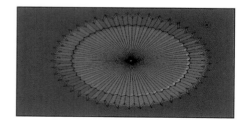

Models for Beginners

Step 16: This wrapper mesh is coming along well. Observe the spikes on the top; those are not actually there on the wrapper, just the peanut butter cup itself. These need to be flattened out. Hit 1 on the numpad. Turn Limit Selection to Visible **Off** and select all of the top vertices.

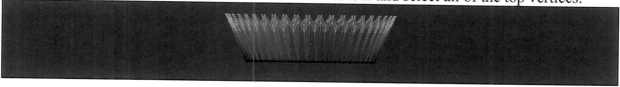

With the vertices selected, hit S to Scale, then Z, and then 0 on the numpad to flatten everything out.

Once the wrapper is done, tab into Object Mode and add a Material to it. Under diffuse, place the color wheel pointer onto the yellow area and turn the slider down to almost totally black, but not completely down. Also, set the Specular Level to .091 to reduce the reflectivity.

It looks good, leave it at that!

Step 17: While in Object Mode, hit ALT + H to unhide the peanut butter cup. Once both are visible, make sure the wrapper is selected and tab into Edit Mode. No help will be given to you at this point. Your job is is to position the wrapper closely around, but not too closely to the peanut butter cup. This will take a bit of grabbing and scaling (on a single axis). Then check it. Is it ok? How do test renders (F12) look from different angles. Don't rush this part. Take you time and get it positioned well! Yours should look similar to this.

Step 18: Once positioned, the meshes should not be joined, but parented. Go into Object Mode. Select the peanut butter cup first, then the wrapper: Hit CNTRL + P and parent them. In this case, the wrapper becomes the parent, as it is easier to grab and move the exterior (wrapper) part of the mesh when wanting to reposition. Additionally, make a non-linked duplicate of the the wrapper and peanut butter cup while in Object Mode.

Step 19: We need something for the peanut butter cups to sit on. While in Object Mode, add a plane, tab into Edit Mode, and scale the plane up to situate it under the peanut butter cups. Extrude the back end up into a quarter pipe and then hit the Smooth button under Shading (not Smooth Vertex).

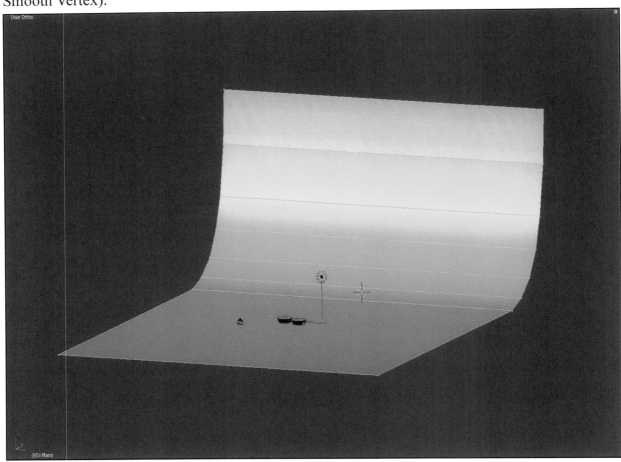

Finally, go to the Material tab and add a material, but don't do anything else.

Step 20: Render time! Position the scene and camera (CNTR + ALT + 0) and do a quick render. For mine, Environment lighting was turned on. Please do the same by checking it in the world tab.

It looks good, but not exactly perfect. Currently, Environment lighting is on, with one light (the default) above it. Duplicate the existing light and move it over to the left. With this new light selected, go to the lamp tab on the right and click on no shadow.

Once that is done, another problem has to be solved. The wrappers are not lit well. You took all that time putting ridges in them, and they can't be seen. Do it quick n' dirty. Duplicate two more lamps and place one in front of each peanut butter cup. Your lighting scene should look as such.

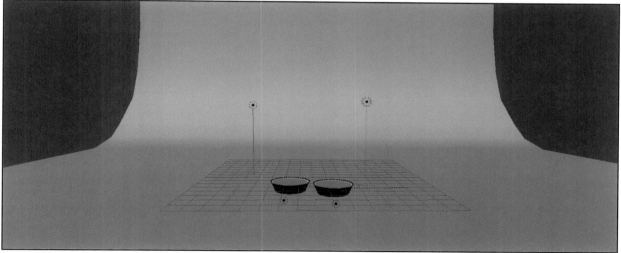

Do another render. See next page.

Much better. Leave it at that.

Discussion:

First off, this model turned out very well. The first area of concern is the 2 front lights creating a reflection at the bottom, but this only adds character to the scene. Yeah, it actually looks better with them there. If in a differing situation with reflection not being desired, a different lighting setup could be used for the front or the Specular Level of the plane texture could be reduced to Zero.

As stated before, nothing much has to be done to this model, -it looks good. For those wanting some additional realism, some tweaks can be made. For the wrapper, some addition loop cuts around the edges could be added. The with these new vertices, the wrapper could be peeled back a little in certain areas. This is how objects in real life oftentimes are: THEY ARE NOT PERFECT. This lack of perfection makes them more believable.

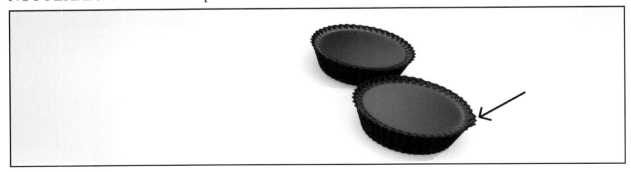

Models for Beginners

The same can be done with the crimped edges of the peanut butter cup. In real life, they are not this perfect. The idea is to move a few slightly, but not to be drastic about it. Be extremely subtle.

Model 3: Golf Ball (Easy)

Step 1: Start with a new scene, and hit X to delete the cube. Add → Mesh → Icosphere, and at the bottom left, set the subdivisions to 4.

Step 2: Go to the Modifiers tab and add a Bevel Modifier. The default width value of .1 should be left, and immediately click Apply. Tab into Edit Mode and hit A to deselect the entire mesh.

Step 3: Click face select and make sure Limit Selection to Visible is **On**. Hit 1 on the numpad This should be your mesh.

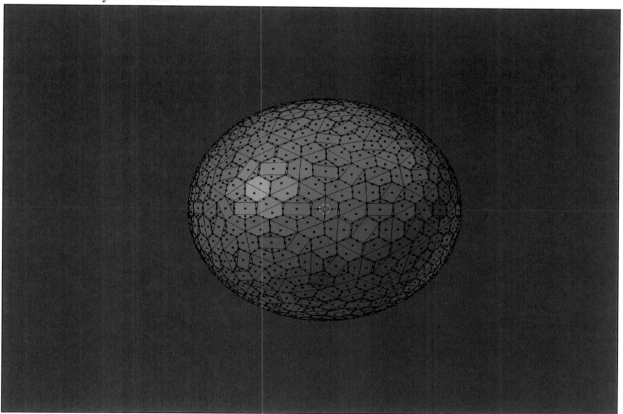

Look closely at the mesh, a bevel has been added. Notice how it is not equal all the way around. It is very slim at the bottom. So slim in fact that it looks almost like one line. There is face however!

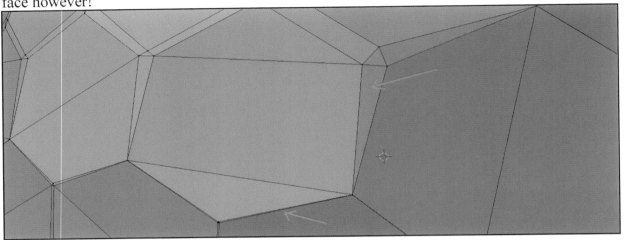

Step 4: Time to make the dimples. Click on Face Select Mode, and the idea here is to select everything but the bevels. However, there is a shortcut for doing this. First, select 2 of the inner faces, but do not select the bevel surrounding them.

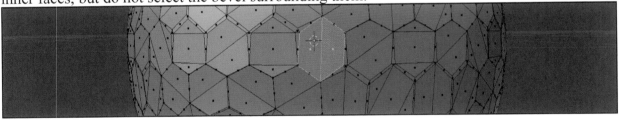

Then hit SHFT + G and select Area. This should have happened.

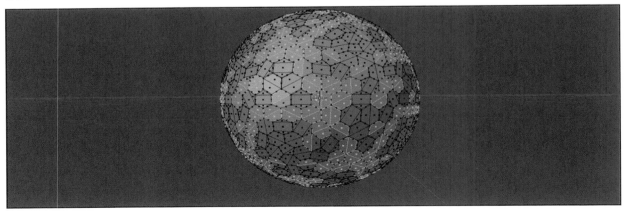

This is the 'Select Similar' feature in action, but notice that it did not select them all. That is ok, the procedure just needs repeating. Select 2 more faces (a couple can be done at once), but don't select any of the faces making up the bevels. Again, hit SHFT + G and select area. Keep going until they are all selected.

This should be what your mesh looks like when finished.
Note: The last couple may need to be selected by hand.
Be sure to check the mesh over thoroughly; spin it up and down, then left and right. Over and over again.

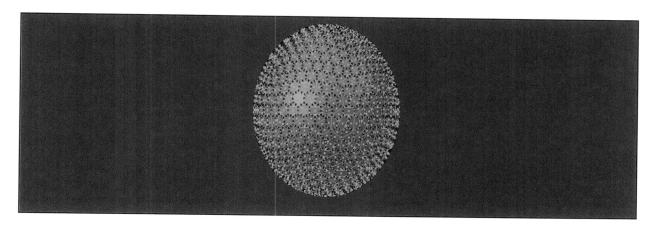

Did you get all of them selected?

Step 7: Yes, a nice golf ball will be made out of this strangeness, just hang on. First, switch the pivot point to the 3D cursor.

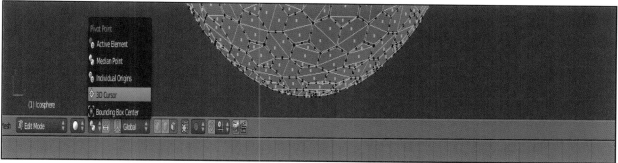

The only other matter of importance is to make sure the 3D cursor is in the center of the mesh. If it is not, Hit SHFT + S, → Cursor to Center.
Step 8: Hit E to extrude, then immediately left click to finalize. Hit S, and scale in the very slightly.

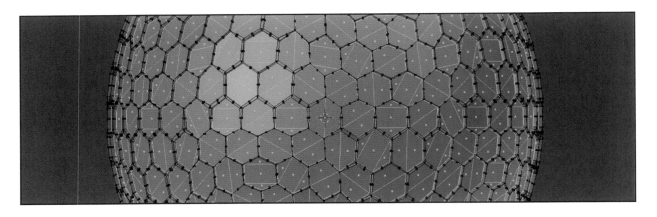

Step 9: Switch the pivot point to Individual Origins. This will allow for scaling along the normals.

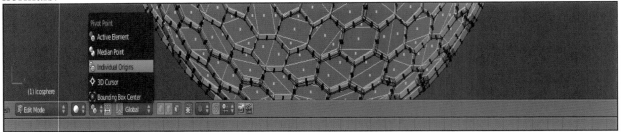

Now scale in a bit. Don't go crazy, just a bit. You will know that it is about right when some of the scaled faces take the shape of a coffin!

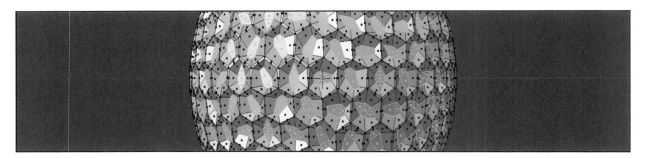

Step 11: Here is the magical part. The ratio of the flat surface area to the dimples is obviously out-of-whack! After all, the flat surface area of real golf balls is obviously wider. This situation can be cleverly rectified. Tap A to deselect the dimples, then hit A to select the entire mesh. In the Tools panel on the left, hit Smooth Vertex 2 times. ***Note: NOT Smooth Shading.***

This should result. See next page.

Wow, the dimples got smaller, and the flat surface became wider. This is exactly what was desired!

Save the file as GolfBall001.

Step 13: Add a Subdivision Surface Modifier and set the **View** and **Render** values to 3. Snap off a quick render with F12
So far, so good.

Step 14: Add a material, and keep the Diffuse value to pure white. Turn the slider on the right all the way up. Finally, set the hardness to 254. For the World settings, set a bluish sky, and click on Blend. Set .25 as the Ambient Occlusion setting. In the Render tab, turn up the Resolution to 100% and check Anti-Aliasing.

Do a final render.

However, the underpart to the left is a little too under-lit. Don't go crazy here, just duplicate the default lamp and move it to the bottom left. Select the lamp and turn the energy down to: .25 and set to No Shadow.

Do another render.

Model 4: Flashlight (Moderate)
Part A (Shaft – Battery Cap - Lanyard Ring)
Step 1: Start with a new scene, X to delete the cube, hit 1 and 5 on the numpad. Add a Tube, and before doing anything else, set the vertices to 24 (this setting is at the bottom of the Tool Shelf on the left). Then tab into Edit Mode.
Step 2: With the tub selected, hit S, then Z, and scale the tube up 14 units.
Step 3: The batter cap will now be made. Hit 2 on the numpad once, then select the entire bottom using the B key.

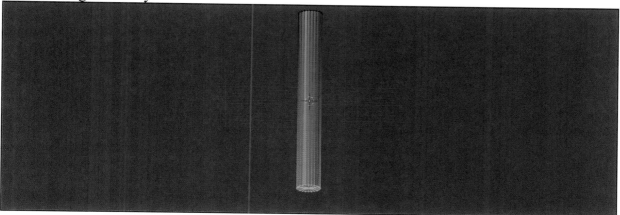

Step 4: Hit E to extrude, and make one very small extrusion and then left click to finalize.

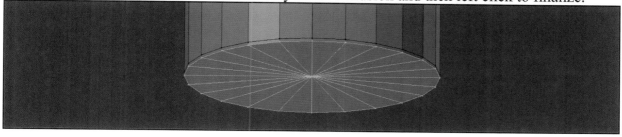

Step 5: Hit E again, then Z, and make a larger extrusion.

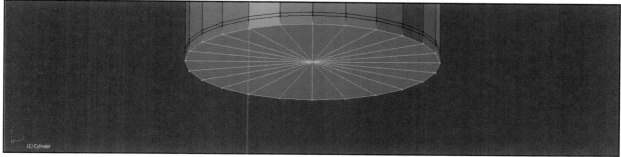

3D Modeling

Step 6: Make one final extrusion for the entire battery cap. Left click to finalize. Tap A when done.

Here is a full view showing all of the extrusions.

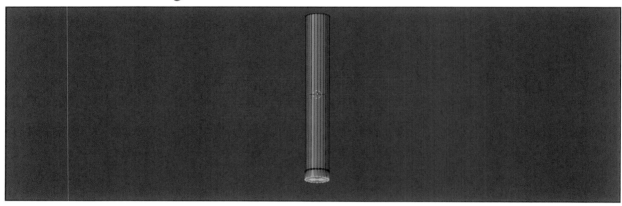

Step 7: Zoom in on a first extrusion, hit CNTRL + R, and place 3 loop cuts between the existing loops. Tap A when finished.

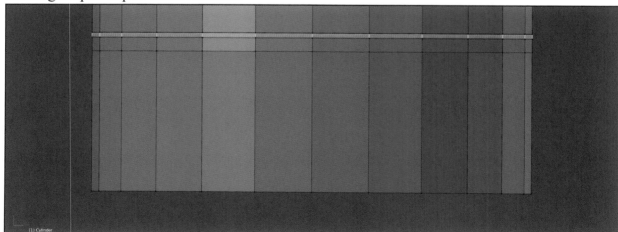

Step 8: Hit ALT and right click on the very center loop.

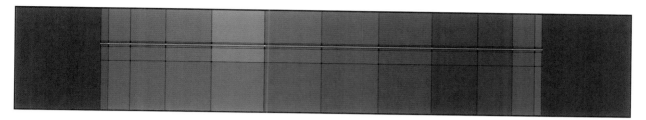

Hit S and scale in a bit.

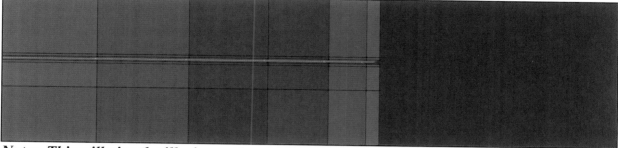

Note: This will give the illusion, at least when viewed from a distance, that the battery cap is a separate object screwed into the base. This technique is a great little time saver, and it works flawlessly in most cases.

Step 9: Great, hit 2 on the numpad twice, and select the following vertices.

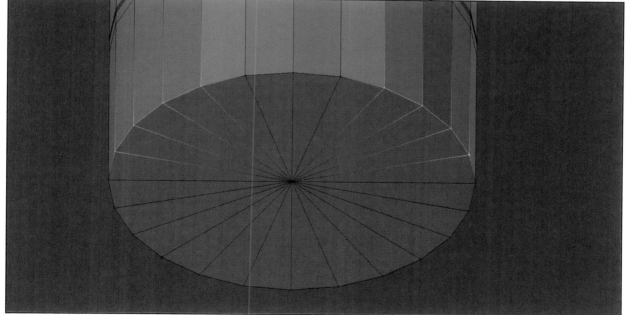

Hit X and delete the vertices.

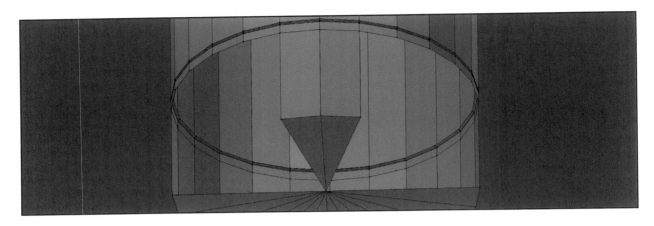

Step 10: Switch to Edge Select Mode, and select the following 3 edges (the last one is white).

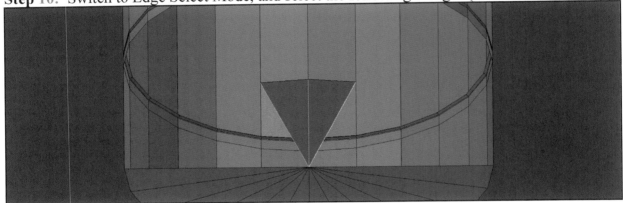

Hit X and delete the Edges (not the vertices).

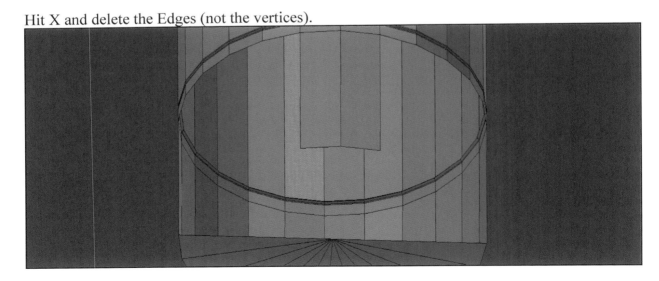

Step 11: Carefully select the following two vertices.

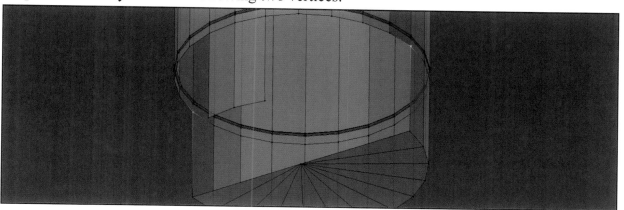

Hit F to fill, then hit W and subdivide twice. Three vertices should have been added.

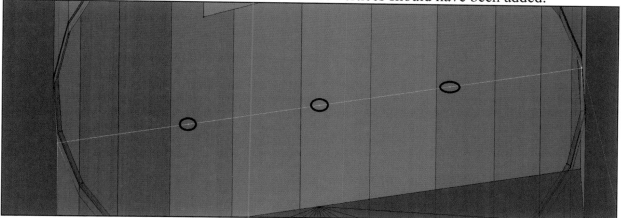

Step 12: Tap A to deselect everything, and now select the following 3 vertices.

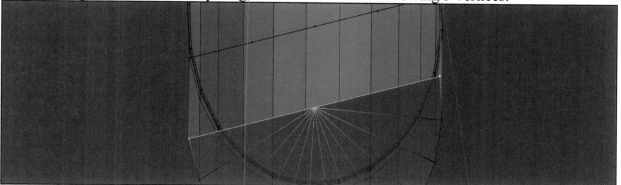

3D Modeling

Hit W and subdivide once. Two additional vertices will be added. Tap A when done.

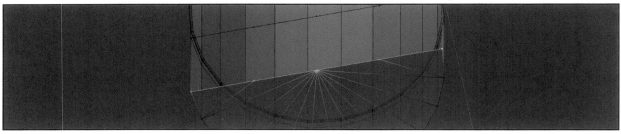

Step 13: Select the 4 vertices shown.

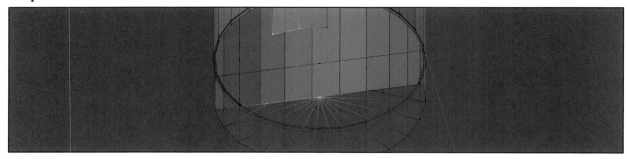

Then Hit F to fill.

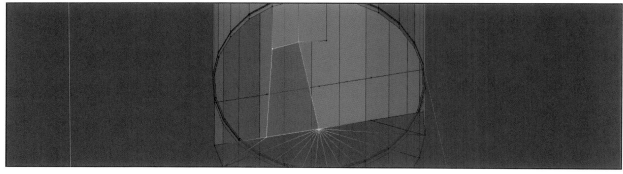

Do the same procedure for the right side. The result is shown below.

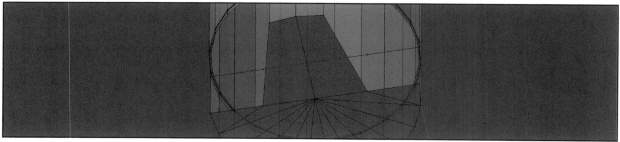

Step 14: Select the following 3 vertices.

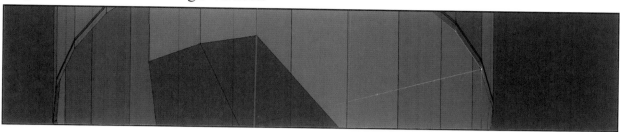

Then F to Fill

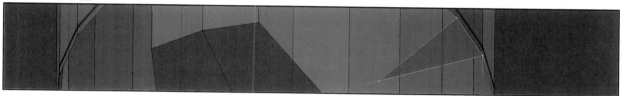

Step 15: Continue on with the next 3 vertices and fill.

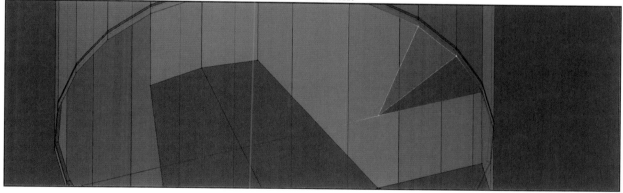

Step 16: Continue in the same manner and fill the next 3 triangles.
*Note: **Do not use the middle vertex (shown in black circle) to make the triangles. The triangle points should all come off the single vertex shown in green.***

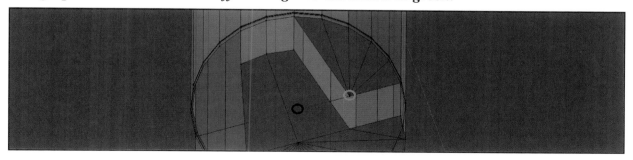

3D Modeling

Step 17: Select the following 4 vertices.

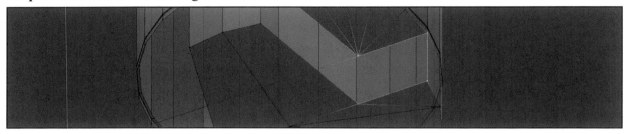

And fill with F.

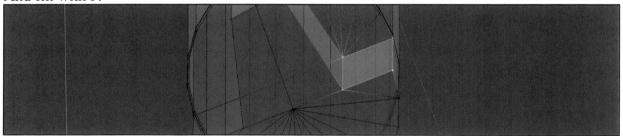

Step 18: Select the following 4 vertices.

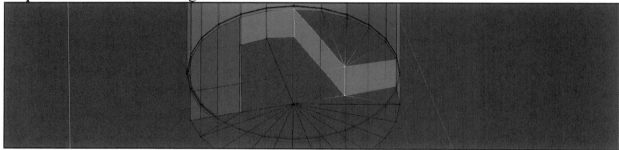

And F to fill.

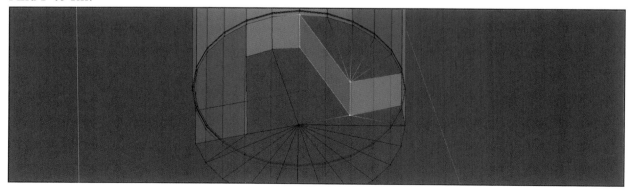

Step 20: Repeat this filling procedure for the other side. The finished result is shown below.

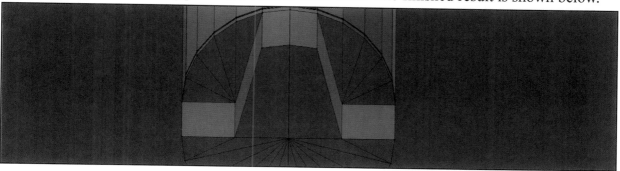

Step 21: Switch to Edge Select Mode. Select both of the shown edges (hold SHFT for the second one (the one on the right is highlighted in white)).

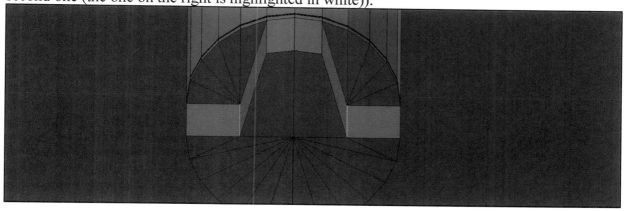

Hit S to scale, then X and scale in as shown on the next page.

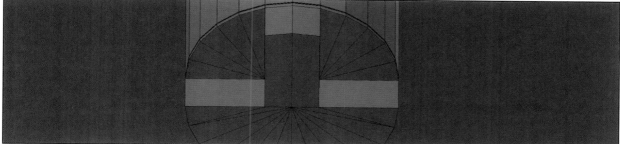

Note: This concludes Part A of the flashlight tutorial.
Save the file (FlashLight001), and take a break if needed.
Part B Lanyard hole
Step 1: Switch to Face Select Mode, and select the following face.

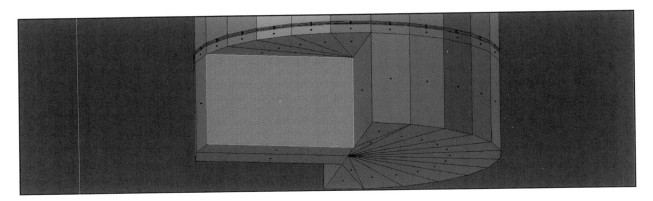

Step 2: Hit E to extrude, then immediately left click to finalize the extrusion. Hit S to scale, then .7 on the numpad. Left click when finished.

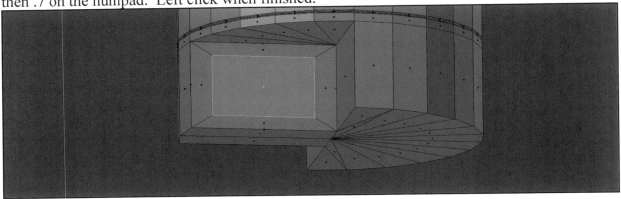

Step 3: With the newly created face still selected, hit W and subdivide 1 time. Tap A when finished.

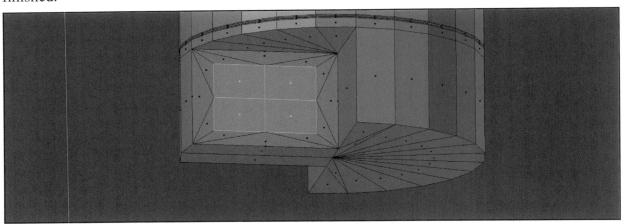

Step 4: Switch to Vertex Select Mode, and select the following vertex.

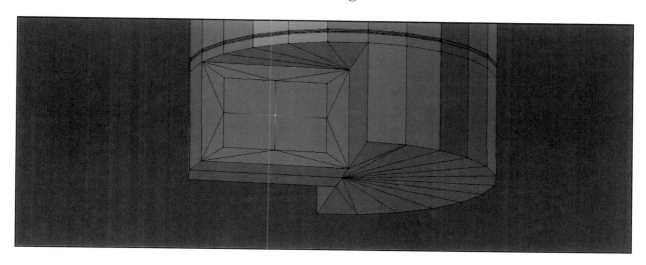

Hit X and delete the vertex.

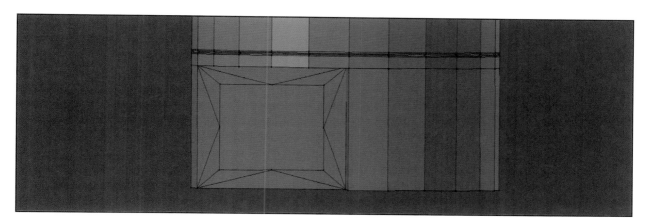

Step 5: Select the following vertices.

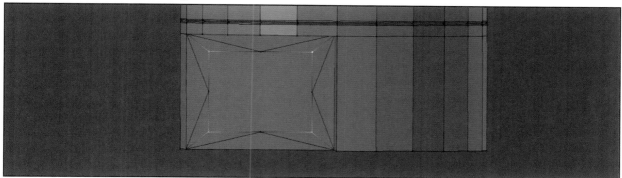

Hit S to scale, then .7 on the numpad, then left click.

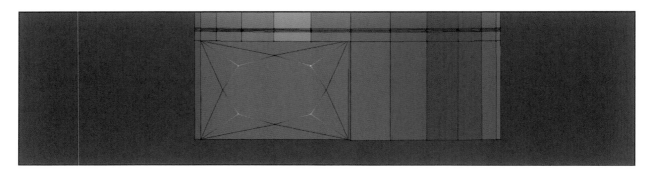

Step 6: Select the following vertices.

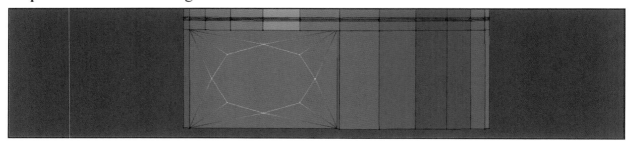

Hit S, then 1.2 on the numpad to enlarge it slightly.

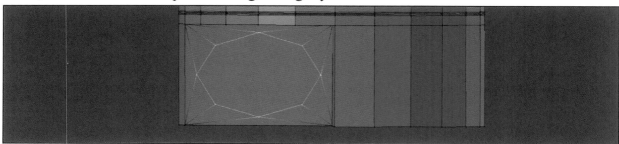

Step 7: Do the same for the reverse side.

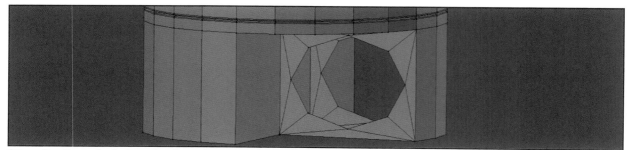

Step 8: Start knitting the interior together. Select 4 vertices that line up, and hit F to fill.

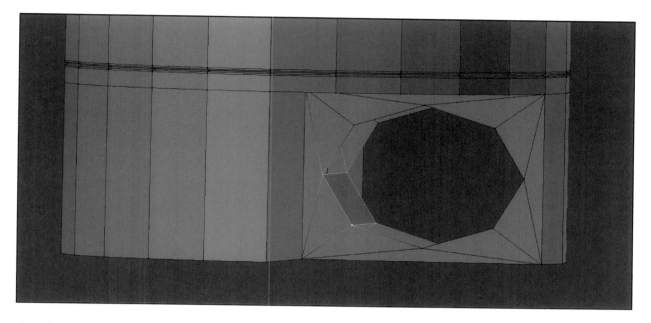

Continue around the interior until the whole interior is filled. The final result is shown in perspective view.

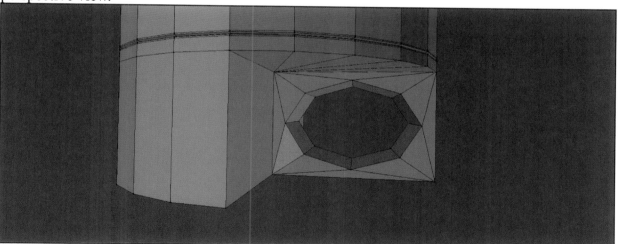

Note: This concludes Part B of the flashlight tutorial. Save the file as Flashlight002, and take a break if needed.

Part C, Flashlight Head, Smoothing, and Lens

Step 1: Lets start with the flashlight head. Hit 1 on the numpad, and select the top loop using ALT + Right Click. Make Sure the center vertex on the top is not selected. All that is needed is the top loop. See next page for picture.

3D Modeling

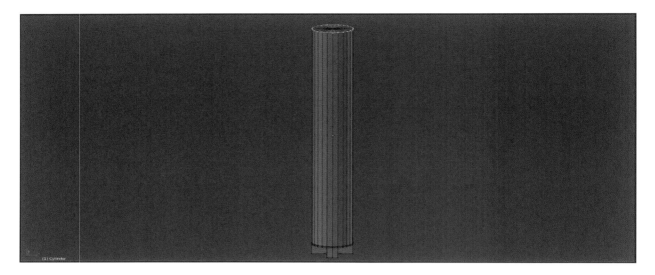

Step 2: Hit 1 on the numpad, zoom in, hit E to extrude, then immediately left click to finalize. Hit S and scale out slightly.

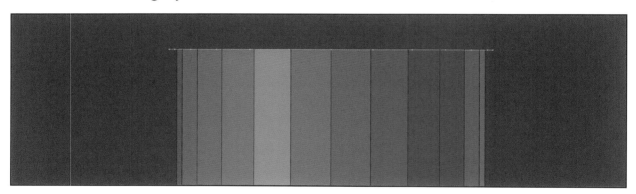

Step 3: Hit E and extrude down just a little.

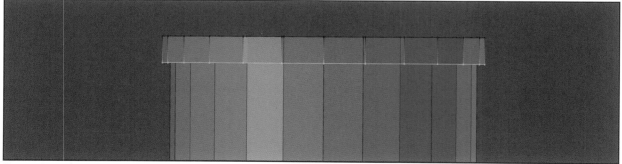

Step 4: Hit E to extrude, then left click to finalize it. Scale out a little.

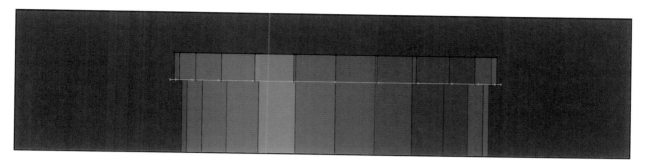

Step 5: Zoom out, so the entire flashlight can be seen. Hit E, and extrude up about 3.5 units.

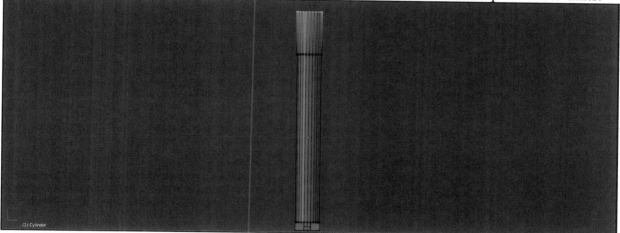

Step 6: Add 6 loop cuts to the flashlight head by hitting CNTR + R and scrolling the mouse wheel.

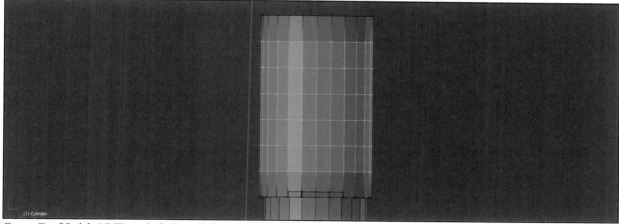

Step 7: Hold ALT and right click on the top loop.

Then hold SHFT + ALT and right click on the 2 below.

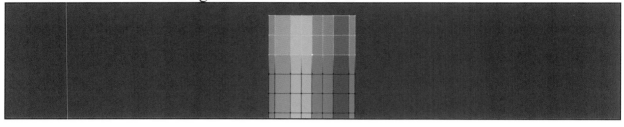

With the 3 loops selected. Hit S to scale, then 1.5 on the numpad. Left click to finalize. Tap A when done.

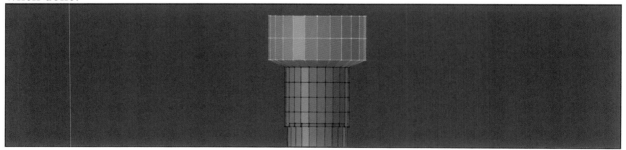

Step 9: Holding ALT, right click on the 4th loop down.

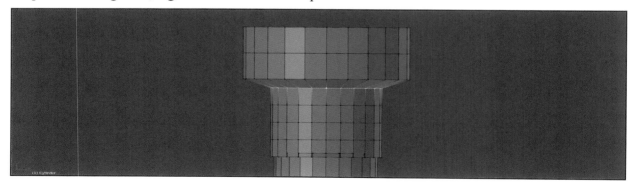

Hit S to scale, then 1.4 on the numpad. Left click to finalize.

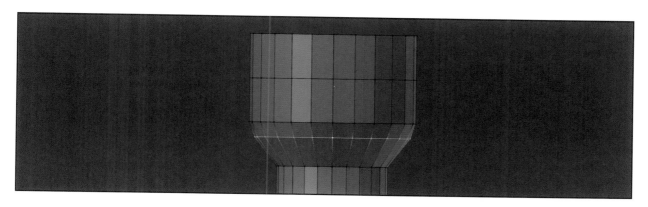

Step 10: Repeat this procedure for the next 3 loops down. Use the values of 1.3, 1.2, and 1.1.

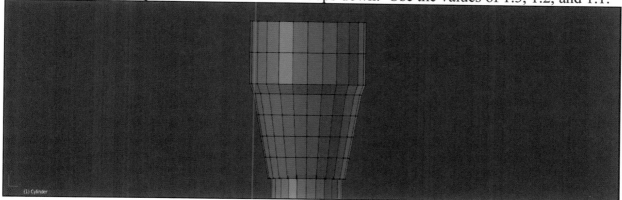

Step 11: Everything is fine, but the loop spacing is obviously off. Select the 3rd loop down, hit G and move it up a little. Tap A when done.

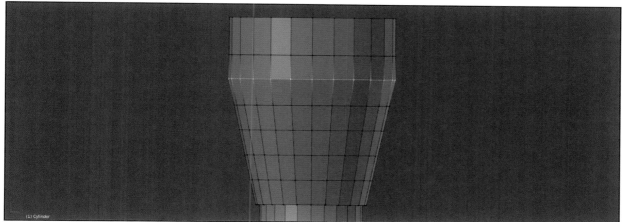

Step 12: Hit 8 on the numpad 3 times and select the top loop.

Step 13: Hit E to extrude, then immediately Left Click to finalize. Hit S and scale in a little.

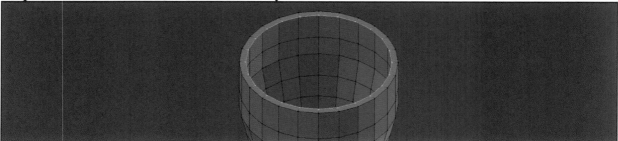

Step 14: Hit 1 on the numpad, switch to Wireframe Mode. Hit E and extrude down a little.

Hit S and scale it in.

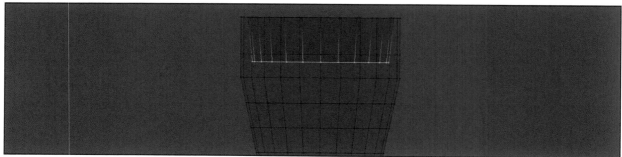

Step 15: Continue down 3 more extrusions with scaling. On the last one, hit W and Merge at Center. The end result should look similar to this.

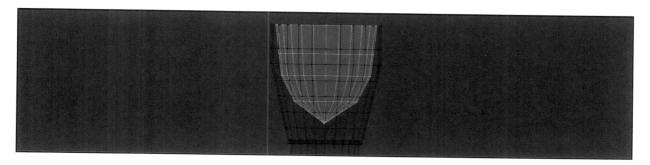

Here is a shaded bird's eye view.

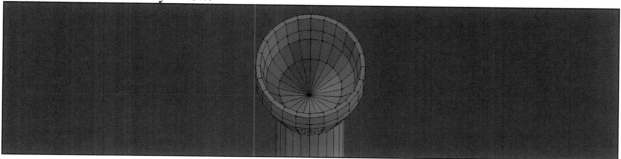

Step 16: Add a Subdivision Surface modifier, and set 4 for the **View** and **Render** levels. Do NOT apply the modifier. Zoom in on the batter cap. Add a controlling loop (CNTRL + R) to curtail the smoothing.

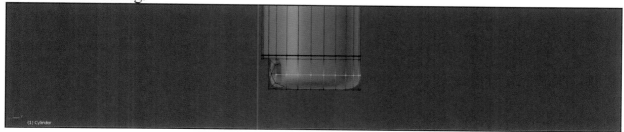

Left click and slide it down.

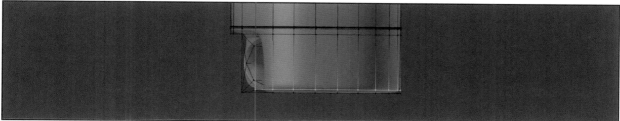

Step 17: The outer portion of the key ring loop is an ugly mess.

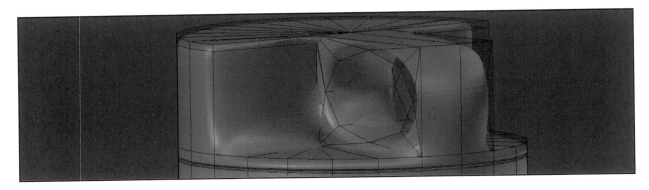

Add a control loop (CNTR + R) and slide it into the following position.

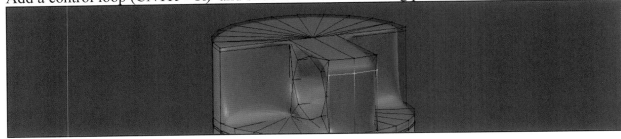

add another here,

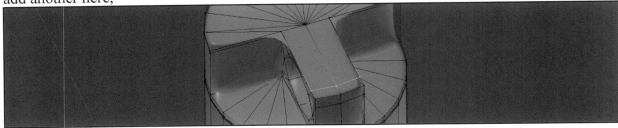

add another here.

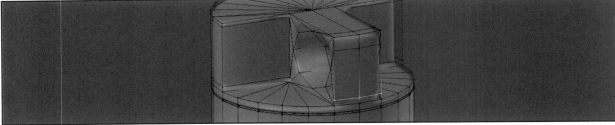

Step 18: The inside of the key ring also needs 2 controlling loops. Place the first one on the left. Shown in Wireframe Mode.

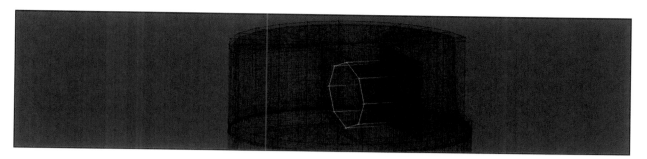

And one on the right.

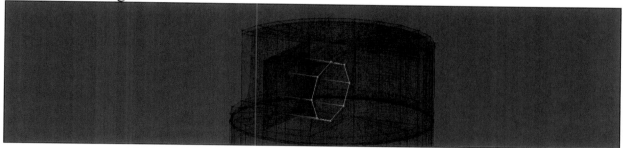

Step 19: Place one final controlling loop here.

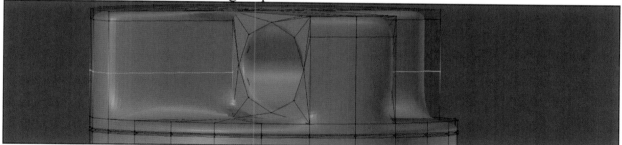

And slide it down.

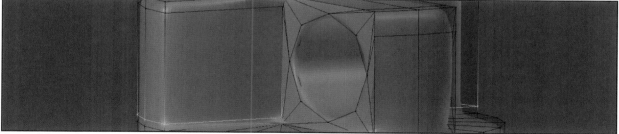

Step 20: The next area to calm down is the head. The top part is too sharp.

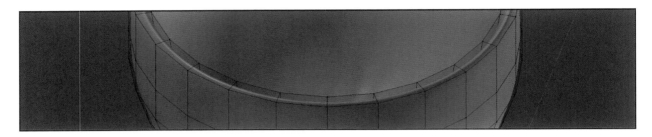

Place 2 controlling loops to square it off. The first:

And the second:

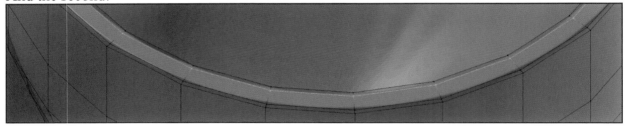

Step 21: Great, the last step is to add the lens. Tab into Object Mode (this makes the lens a separate object from the flashlight), and add a circle. Immediately check the fill box. Do not position the lens at this time.

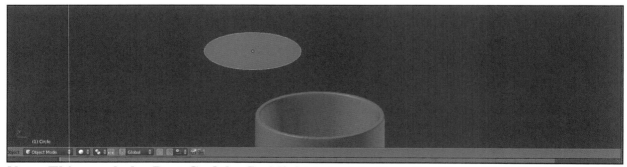

Note: This concludes Part C of the flashlight tutorial. Save the file as Flashlight003. and take a break if needed.

Part D, Materials, Lighting, and Rendering

Step 1: Select the flashlight, and tab into Edit Mode. Tap A and select the entire flashlight. and click on the Material button. Under Diffuse, select a nice blue (your choice), and to create an anodized look, set the specular value to 0.8. The blue material should automatically assign itself. Below is the result in Object Mode.

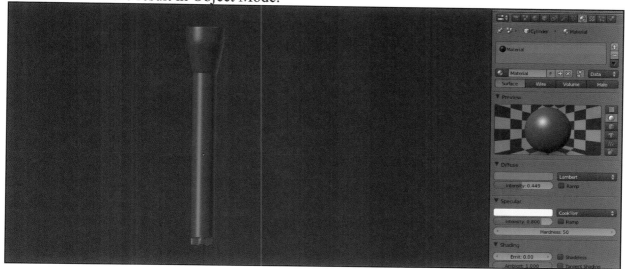

Step 2: Time to colorize the inner head. Make certain to be in Edit Mode. Deselect the flashlight by hitting A, switch to Face Select Mode, hit 7 on the numpad. Turn on Limit Selection to Visible **On**. Select the inner faces of the Flashlight head with Circle select (C key).

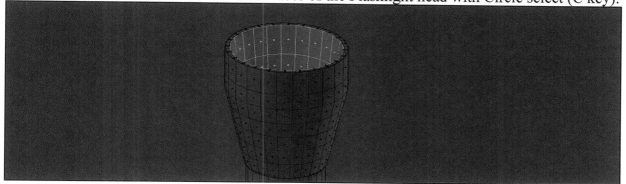

Step 3: With the inner head selected, go to the Material tab, Click the plus at the top (shown with a red circle).

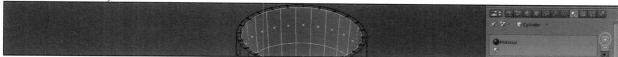

then hit the New button. Select a bright white, and set 1.0 as the specular value. Hit the Assign button. Great, that takes care of the coloration.

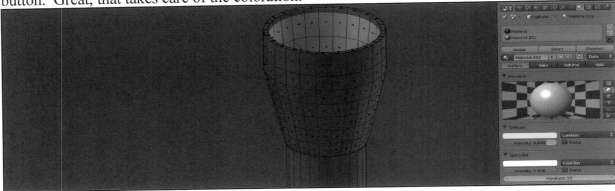

Step 4: Now for the lens. Tab into Object Mode, select the lens and tab back into Edit Mode. Scale and position the lens to fit into the head.
Note: If problems with scaling occur, hit SHFT + S, and select Cursor to Selected.

Step 5: With the lens selected, add a material. Select Transparency, then click the Raytrace button. Turn the Alpha down to 0. Finally, give it an IOR value of 1.5. These values will make the lens appear as glass with a slight reflective property. Better still, you will be able to actually look through the glass and see the highly reflective inner part of the head.

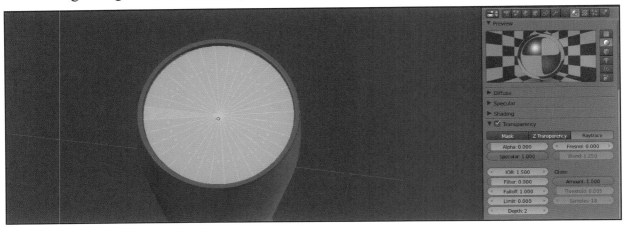

Step 6: For the bulb itself, nothing will be made, but a lamp will be placed inside the head. Tab into Object Mode, and duplicate the lamp in the scene with SHFT + D. Center the lamp inside the head using 1, 3, and 7 on the numpad for centering.

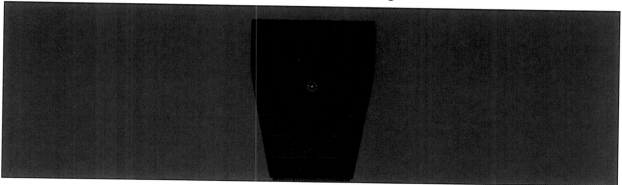

Step 7: Next is to place a Spot lamp right in front of the flashlight. This will actually be seen as an emitting light. Add → Lamp → Spot. In the settings, under Spot Shape, set the size to 17 and check Halo.

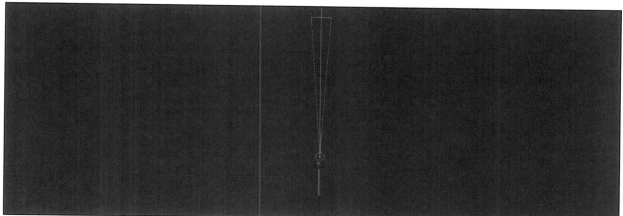

Slide (G key) the light down to make the cone line up with the heads circumference.

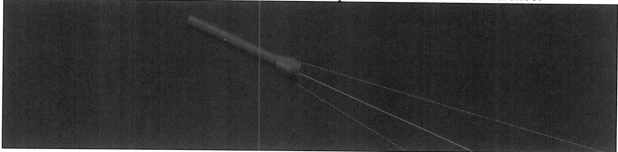

Step 8: In order to get the lamps to move with the flashlight, -they, along with the lens, must be parented. Select the spot light, the lens, and the interior lamp being used as the bulb, then select the flashlight. Hit CNTR + P and parent all of them. When the flashlight is moved they should all move with it.
Note: As an alternative, each of the items can be parented to the flashlight separately.

Step 9: Set the scene up for a quick render. Set the render resolution up to 100% and check Anti-Aliasing. Position some lamps and turn on a little Ambient Occlusion in the World settings. F12 for a rendered shot!

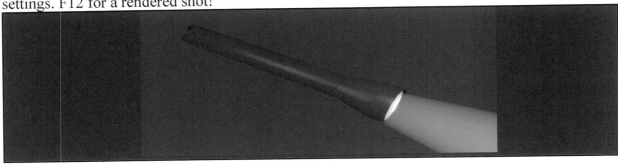

The flashlight looks about how a flashlight should look. However, the endcap does not appear as though it is screwed on. The little scaling trick on the loop did not create enough of an effect. This must be fixed. Select the flashlight and tab back into Edit Mode and hit 1 on the numpad. With Limit Selection to Visible **Off**, select the series of loop cuts which were used to create the separation effect via scaling.

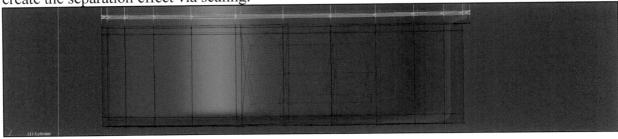

And slide them upwards just a little.

Instead of selecting 1 ring an scaling it in, select 2 and make the scaling more pronounced. This should make it easier to see in the final render.

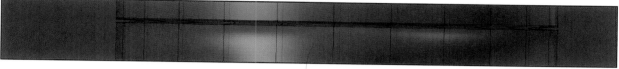

As one final tweak, add 2 additional controlling loops.

The first

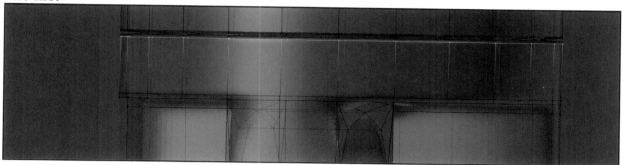

The second

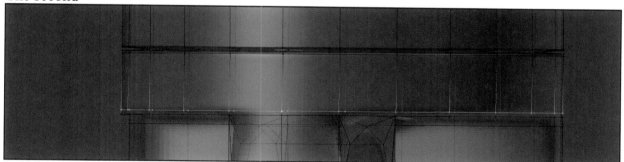

After tabbing into Object Mode, the result is clearly improved.

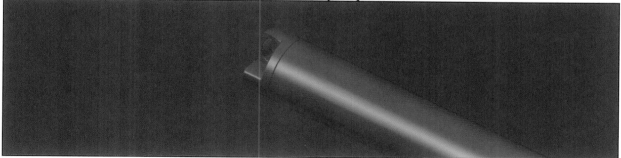

3D Modeling

And one final render with a darkened background to show off the halo effect.

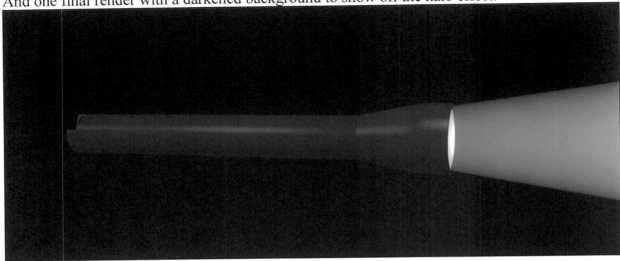

Model 5: USB Flash Drive MP3/Radio Player (Moderate)

Step 1: The metal connector will be built first. Start a new scene, keep the cube, and tab into Edit Mode. Hit 1 on the numpad.

Step 2: Hit S, then X, and scale the cube into a more rectangular shape. As for a measurement, the right and left side of the cube scale ¼ into the the adjacent measurement units.

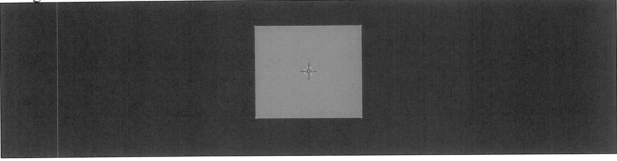

Step 3: Hit 7 on the numpad, then hit S and Y and scale down, as in the picture below. Just get it close to what is seen below.

Models for Beginners

Step 4: It is time to make the rectangular holes in the USB connector. Hit 1 on the numpad, then CNTRL + R and add a vertical loop cut (a little right to center).

Note: As usual, Blender may be making it hard for the loop cut to appear. Keep moving the mouse around when this occurs.

Add another in the position seen below. Again, this can be estimated.

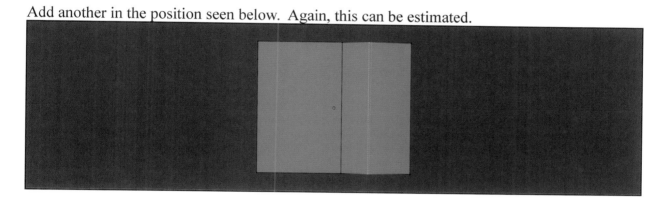

Step 5: Using CNTRL + R, add 2 horizontal loop cuts one-by-one. These must be measured using the grid. The top horizontal loop is 3 blocks down from the top, the second is 8.

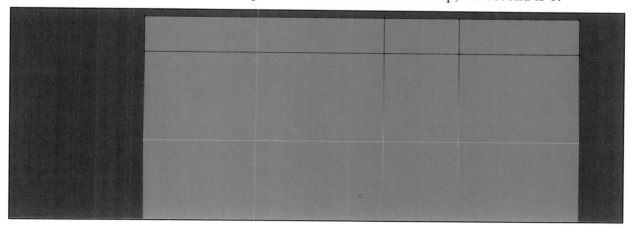

3D Modeling

Step 6: Do the same for the bottom. Keep the measurements equal.

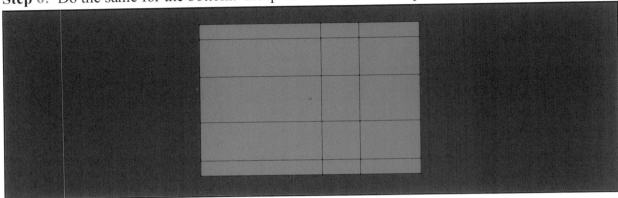

Step 7: Switch to Face Select Mode, hold SHFT and select the 2 shown faces.

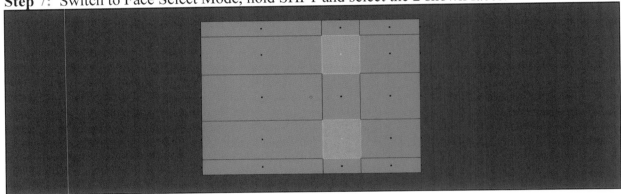

Hit X and delete the faces. Repeat the procedure for the set in the back. This should be the end result.

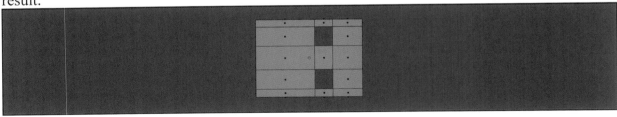

Step 8: Great, hit 3 on the numpad, select the following faces.

Hit X and delete the faces. Do this again to the faces in the back.

This should be the final result.

Step 9: Great, so far, so good. Time to add some tool marks for extra realism. Hit 1 on the numpad, and one-by-one, add the 6 loop cuts (using CNTRL + R) seen in the picture below.

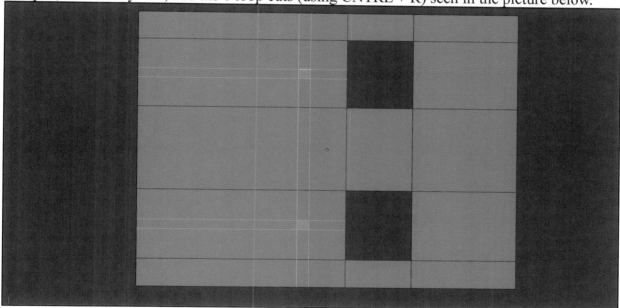

Step 10: Select only the top square.

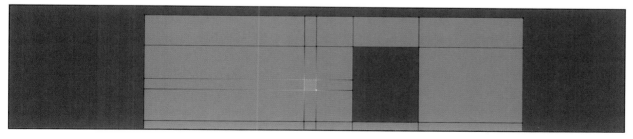

3D Modeling

Then hit E to extrude, and immediately left click to finalize the operation. Then hit S to scale in.

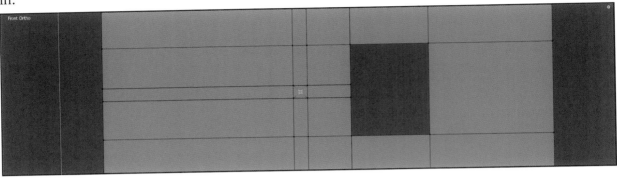

Tap A when done and repeat the procedure for the one below.

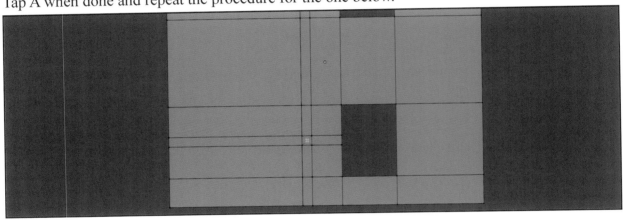

Step 11: It is now time to make the tool-mark indentations. Select both of the inner extrusions.

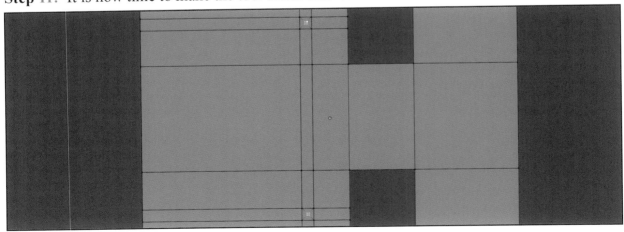

Hit 7 on the numpad and switch to Wireframe. Hit G, then Y and pull up the indentations.

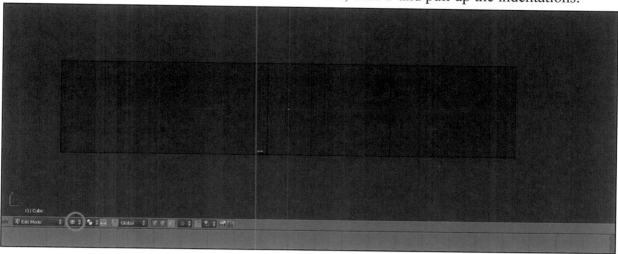

Switch back to Solid shading. This should be the result.

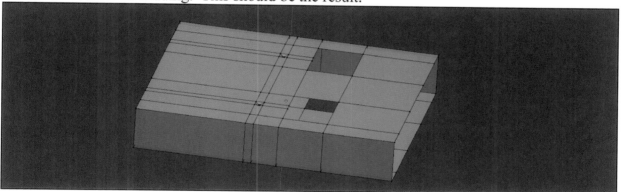

Step 12: Let's make the tabs. Hit 1 on the numpad, then hit CNTRL + R and place a horizontal loop cut dead center. Left click to finalize.

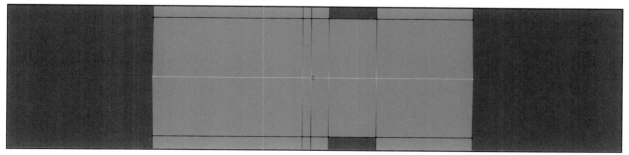

Step 13: Add another one right above it. Roughly 1 unit high.

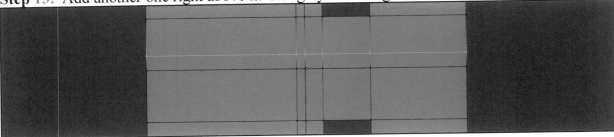

Step 14: Add four vertical loop cuts (one-by-one). Make them 1 unit wide and leave a small gap in between them.

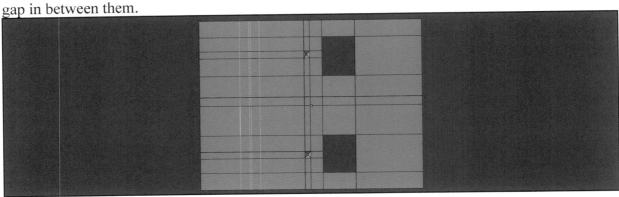

Note: The gap between the two in the middle is very small, -almost hard to see.

Step 15: Add 4 more vertical loop cuts on the right side. Again, make them about 1 measurement unit wide, and leave a small gap between them. Tap the A key when finished.

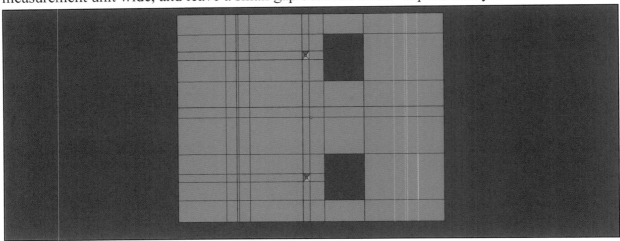

Step 16:   Switch to Face Select Mode and select the following faces.

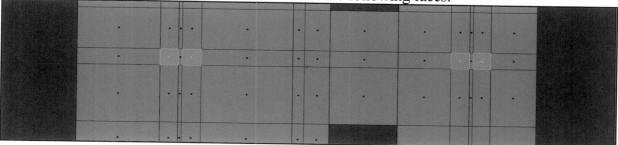

Hit X and delete the faces. The following picture is shown with the background geometry hidden. Yours will look different.

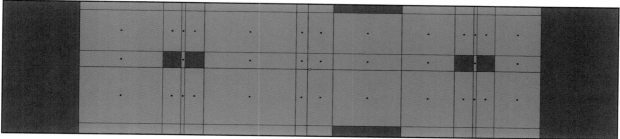

Step 17:   Switch to Edge Select Mode, Hold down SHFT and select all the segments of of middle loop.
Note: Do not hold down ALT and select one segment: It will not work correctly in this situation.

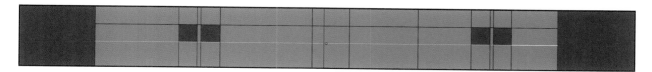

Note: Make sure that you selected all of it. Don't forget the small gaps.

Hit CNTRL + V, and select Rip. Immediately hit X to constrain the axis, and pull down ever so slightly.

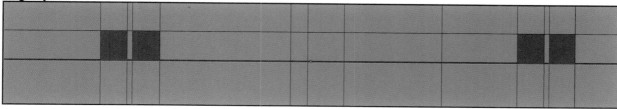

Step 18: Switch to Vertex Select Mode, select the 2 shown vertices and scale in ever so slightly.

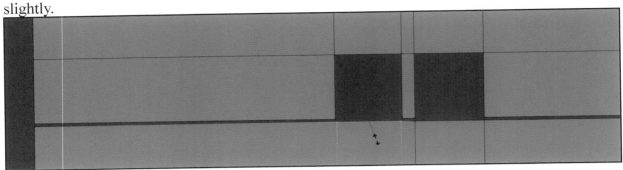

Hit E and extrude up. Keep it tight. The gaps should be very small.

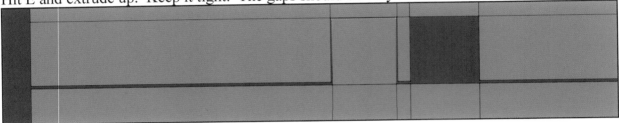

Finish the rest of the tabs. Your result should look similar to this.

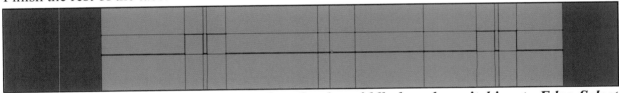

Note: You will most likely have to reselect the the middle loop by switching to Edge Select Mode, and then Hit G, then X to move it up a bit. The idea is to tighten it up. You may also have to go and tweak some of the tabs. Here is a finished picture. Notice how the gap is very small, almost hard to see in some areas.

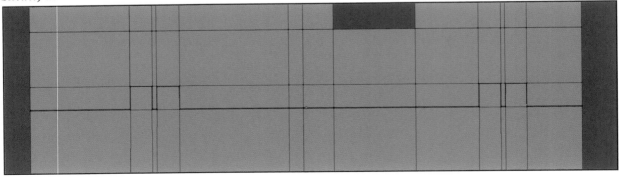

Step 19: The USB connector needs some thickness at this point. The solidify modifier works nicely in this case. Tab into Object Mode, hit 3 on the numpad and click on the the Modifiers button. Click Add Modifier and select Solidify. For the Thickness setting, .01, is just about right. Additionally, put a check beside Even Thickness.

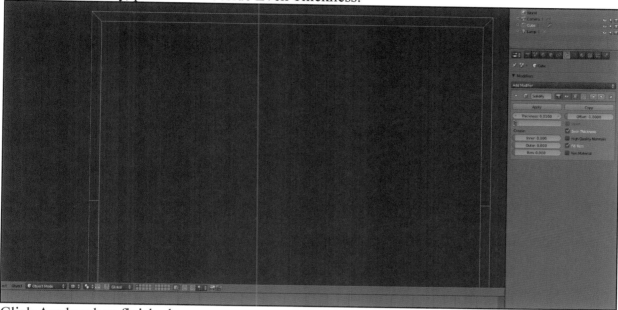

Click Apply when finished.

Step 20: Remember what was said about perfect 90 degree angles; that is a no-no. Stay in Object Mode, hit 1 on the numpad, and Click the Modifier Tab → Add Modifier → then select Bevel. Set the Width to .005 and click Apply. Notice how well it makes the tabs stand out!

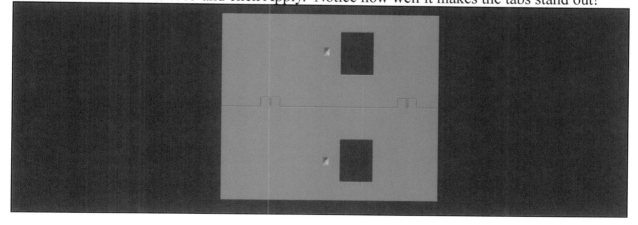

Note: Save the file at this point, USB001.

Step 21: Now is a good time to add the plastic insert. Tab into Object Mode, Add → Mesh → Plane. Zoom out so that the plane can be seen, and click on it to make it the active object. Tab into Edit Mode. Hit R to rotate, then 90 on the numpad. Stick the new plane to the left of the USB connector.

Step 22: This next part is nothing more that adding some thickness and sizing it to fit inside the USB connector. Deal with the thickness first, hit E to extrude, and the Y axis should already be selected. Extrude out one unit or so.

Step 23: Hit 1 on the numpad. Scale on the X, and then the Z axis to make the plastic insert a little smaller than the USB connecter. Here is a hint: Switch to Wireframe mode: Remember, thickness was added. The following should be the result.

Note: Ignore the strange textural effect on the surface. It is an artifact.

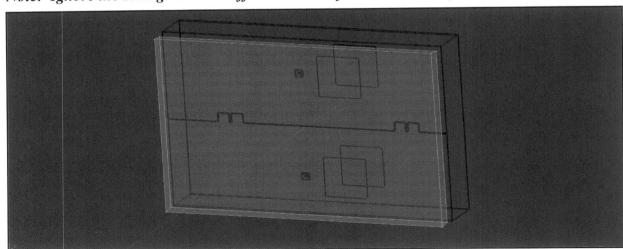

Step 24: The areas for the copper inserts will now be made. Switch the Shading from Wireframe to Solid, and hit 1 on the numpad. Hit CNTRL + R and make 8 horizontal loop cuts by scrolling up the mouse wheel.

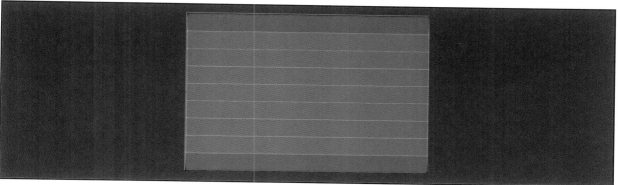

And place 1 vertically (CNTR + R as shown).

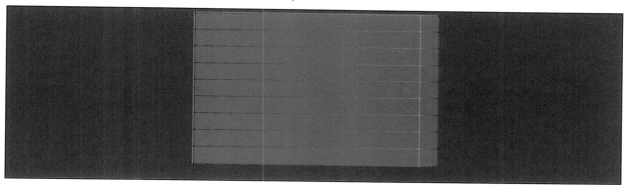

Step 25: We want to make the copper tabs appear to be separate objects. The easiest way to do this is to use the same technique as the flashlight end-cap. Place very tight loop cuts around the entire copper tap. The 2 picture below show the new loop cuts; six in total. Tap A when done.

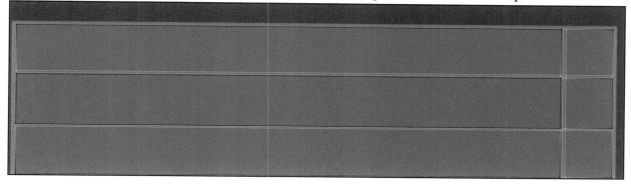

Step 26: Select the middle edge all the way around. Be careful to get all of it.

Tap 4 on the numpad 6 times. Hit G, then Y, and pull them in just a little.

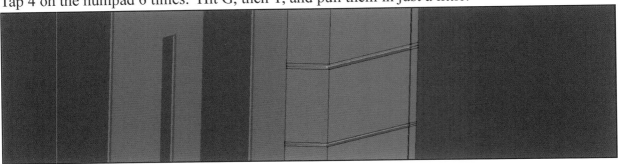

Step 27: Continue on and use this procedure for **every other** one. There will be 4 copper tabs in all.

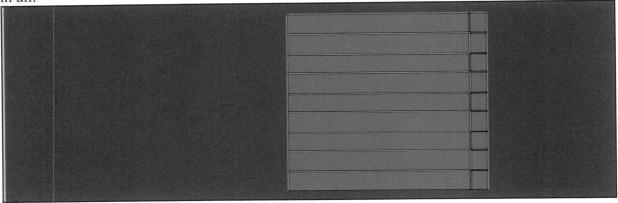

The final result should look as such.

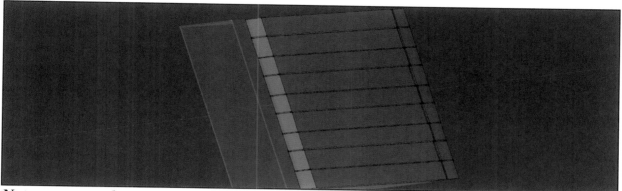

Note, you may also want to grab the 4 copper contacts and move them down ever so slightly, just so they are not on the exact same level as the top.

Step 28: Select the entire insert, and add a Bevel modifier (Width .006).

Note: Save the rile at this point, USB002.

Step 29: As a lucky event, my origin point (orange dot) got away from the insert mesh. It should be roughly in the center. It controls the point from which movement/rotation will occur. This is a common problem with multiple meshes in one scene. Most modelers have no idea how to get it back.

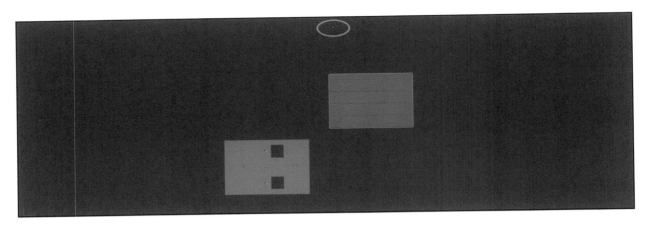

While in Object Mode, click on the Origin button, and select Origin to Geometry. It will go back as such. *Note: **The Origin button is only available in Object Mode.***

Place the insert inside the USB Connector, and leave it there for now.

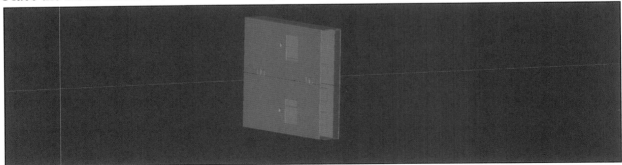

Step 30: It is time to make the body of the USB drive. Tab into Edit Mode, Add → Mesh → Cube. Select it and tab into Edit Mode. Scale (S key) it up on the X axis for a total of 11 units.

Now scale (S key) on the Z axis for a total of 4 units.

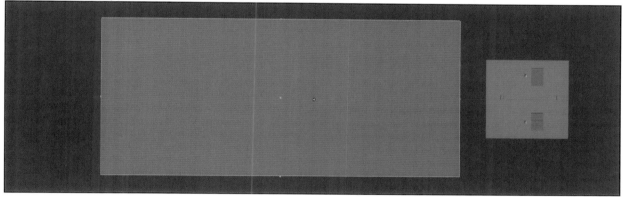

Hit 7 on the numpad, and scale (S key) the width on the Y axis to be 1.5 units high. We want it to be a little sleek!

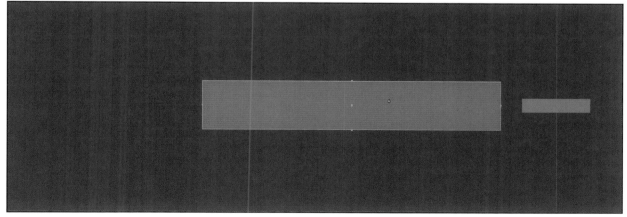

This finishes the scaling.

Step 31: Hit W and Subdivide the body 2 times.

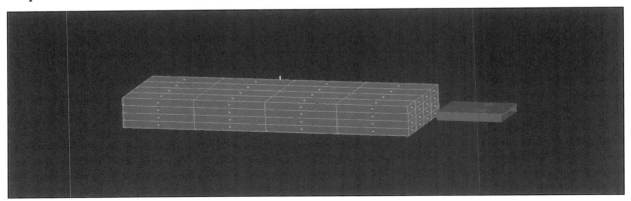

Step 32: Add a Subdivision Surface modifier and Set both the **View** and **Render** levels to 3.

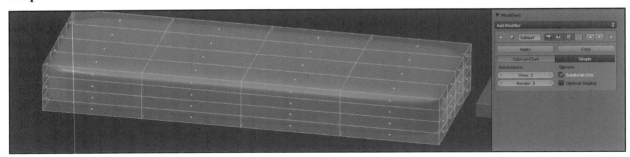

Step 33: Hit G, then X and move the USB drive a little to the left; just to make some room. Select the following faces.

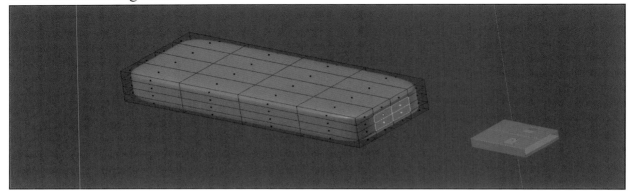

Hit G, then X, and pull them out a little. NOT TOO MUCH.

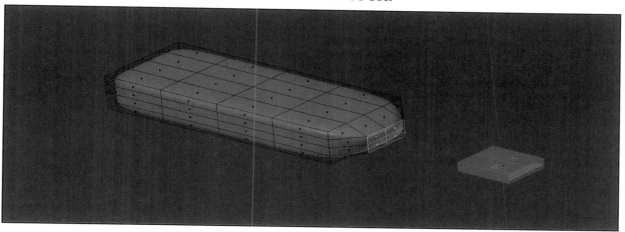

Great, now do the same for the back, but less so. It just needs to be slightly round.

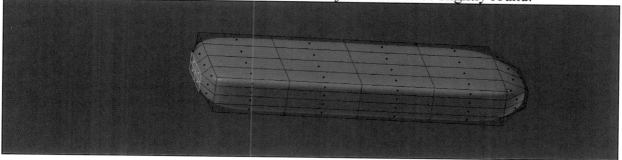

Step 34: Select the entire USB body with the A key. In the Tools panel on the left (hit T if it is not open), click Smooth under Shading.

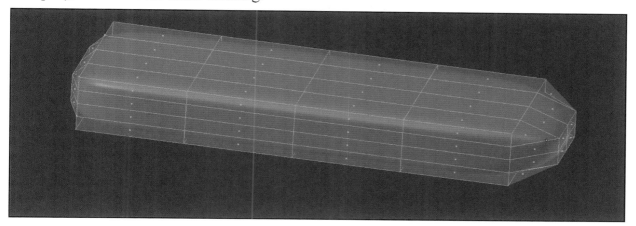

3D Modeling

Note: **Save the file at this point, USB003.**

Step 35: The display screen will now be made. Select the following faces.

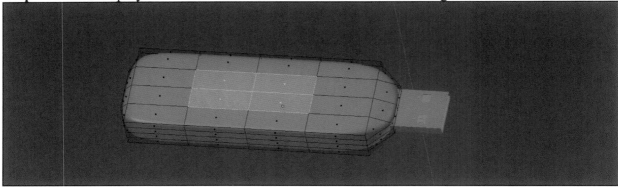

Hit 1 on the numpad, then SHFT + D and duplicate the faces. And pull them up above the USB drive.

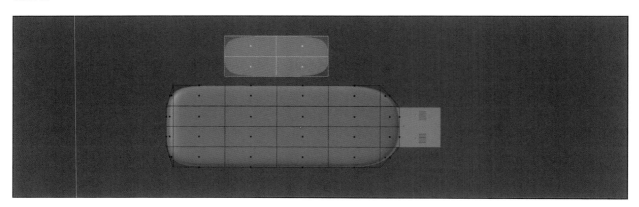

Step 36: Select the same faces again.

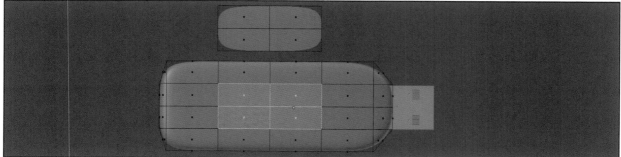

But this time, hit X, and delete faces.

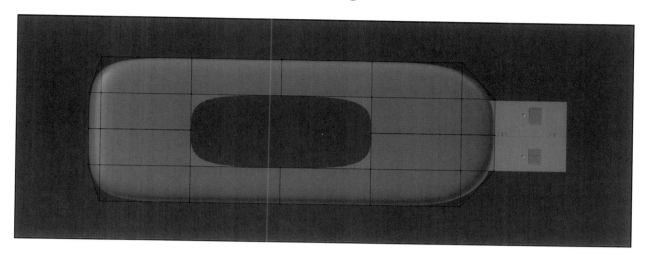

Note: In this picture, the back of the mesh is hidden to make viewing easier. The Subdivision Surface modifier has left the deleted area with rounded edges, for which our newly duplicated screen will fit perfectly. Remember this technique for making a negative when working with the Subdivision Surface modifier.

Step 37: It is time to add the screen text which will emit through the screen. Tab into Object Mode, and Add → Text. (It is under the Add menu, not the Mesh menu). Hit R, X, and then 90 on the numpad.

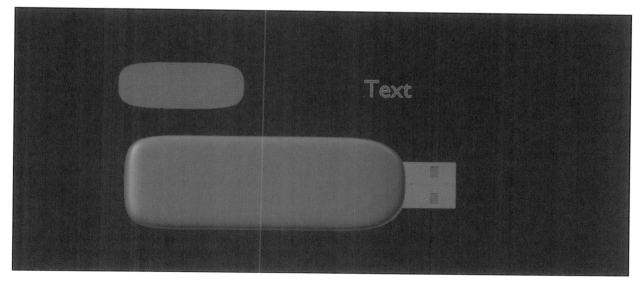

Step 38: Hit 3 on the numpad, and move (G key) the Text object in front of the screen. This is a tilted view.

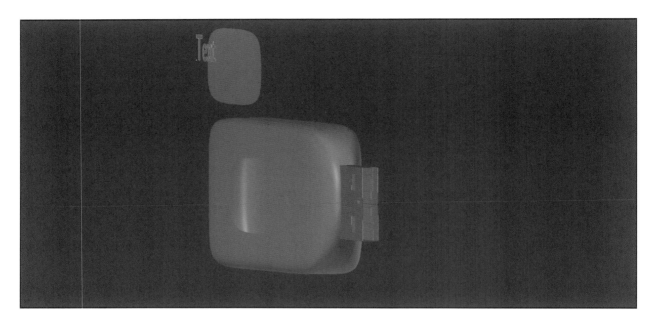

Note: Up to this point, no work has been done with Text objects. They are no big deal, but they do not work like other objects. Their positioning must be done in Object Mode. The Text wording is done in Edit Mode.

Step 39: Click on the Font tab (it newly appears) and set .48 as the Size.

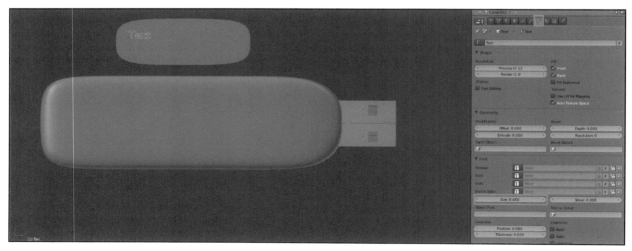

Step 40: As mention before, the Text is being placed in front of the screen for sizing, but there is a problem.

The Text is the same gray color as the screen and will be hard to see. Go to the Materials tab, and place a temporary color on the text. Anything with contrast is acceptable.

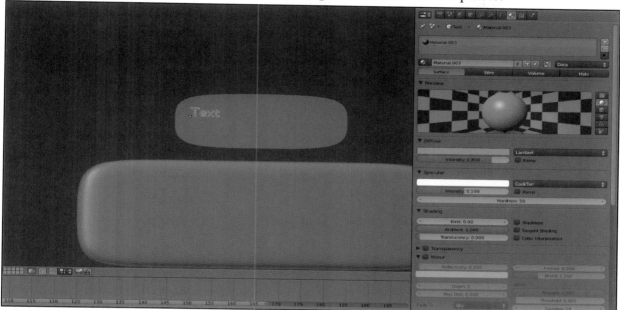

Step 41: Tab into Edit Mode. Here is the fun part. You can type in anything that is desired. I have a volume indicator and then a battery indicator separated by a couple of spaces. Later on, 'strength bars' will be added after each. To get the second line, hit return (as would be the case in any text editor). I added a fictitious radio station call-sign (U.R.A.Y) and 'FM.' Feel free to type whatever you would like.

Step 42: When finished, tab back into Object Mode. The text looks fine, but some extra space could be used between the lines. Go to the Text tab, go down to paragraph, and set 1.4 as the Line value.

Step 43: As one final step with the Text, we want to convert it to a Mesh object. As of now, it is not a mesh, and does not act like a mesh in Edit Mode. Even though no more modifications will be made to the Text, this is still a good idea. Hit Alt + C and select the second option. Tab into Edit Mode and look at the text up close.

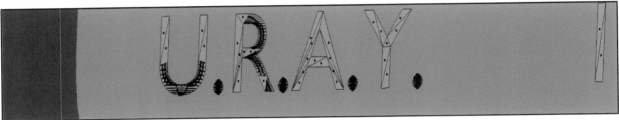

Note: This text can now be modified as a normal Mesh object.

Step 44: The Strength indicators, which are optional, were made by going into Object Mode and adding a plane (Add → Mesh → Plane). They were duplicated and scaled. You should have no problem accomplishing this task.

Note: **Save the file at this point, USB004.**

Step 45: The 1st of 2 controlling pads will now be made, -a thumb joy-stick. While in object mode, select Add → Mesh → Circle. Put a check beside fill. Tab into Edit Mode, Hit R to rotate, X and then 90 on the numpad. Place the circle in front of the USB key. Switch to Edge Select Mode and select the outer edge using ALT.
Note: Do not select the middle vertex.

Models for Beginners

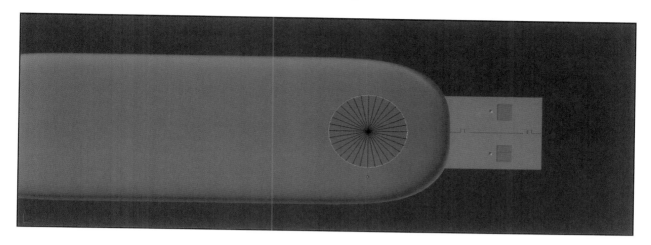

Step 46: Hit 3 on the numpad, then E and extrude down ¼ of a unit on the Y axis. Keep the bottom edge selected for step 47.

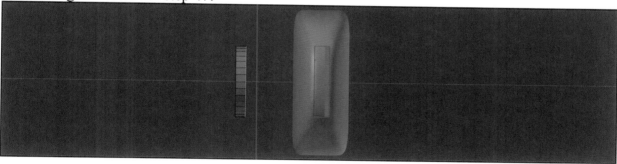

Step 47: The plastic cradle in which the thumb joystick sits, now has to be made. Hit 1 on the numpad. Hit E to extrude, and immediately finalize with a left click. Hit S and scale out just a little.

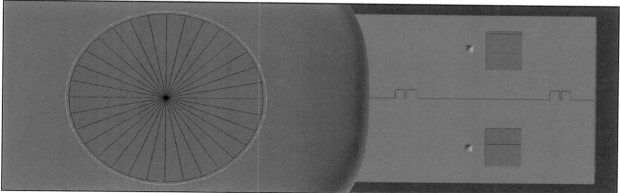

Step 48: Hit 3 on the numpad, then E to extrude just below the top.

♦205♦

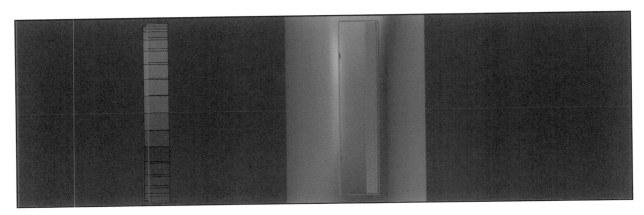

Step 49: Hit 1 on the numpad. Hit E to extrude, then immediately finalize by left clicking. Hit S and scale out a bit.
Note: This extrusion should be larger than the first.

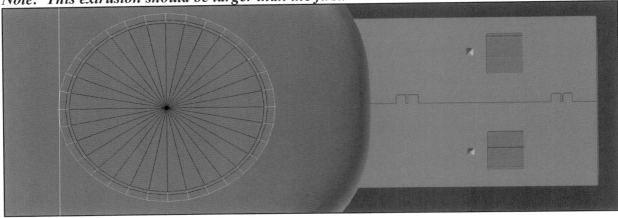

Step 50: Hit 3 on the numpad. Extrude (E key) down a little lower than the base.

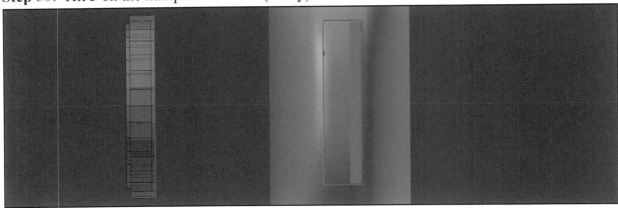

Step 51: Hit 1 on the numpad, and scale (S key) out a little.

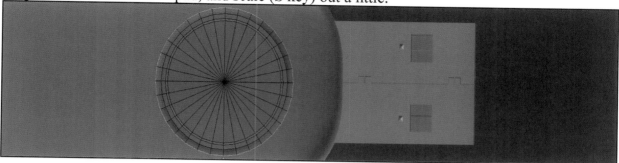

This last scaling created a slant for the cradle's perimeter.

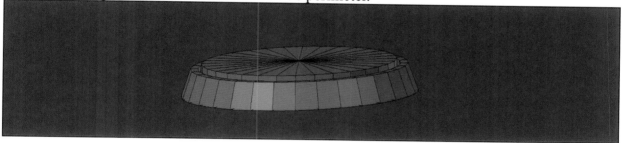

Problem: A concave depression has to be added to the top of the thumb joystick. Here is where the problems start. Instead of modeling it wrong, then doing it right, I'm just going to show you the wrong way, and what results. Most newcomers to modeling would grab the center vertex and pull it down.

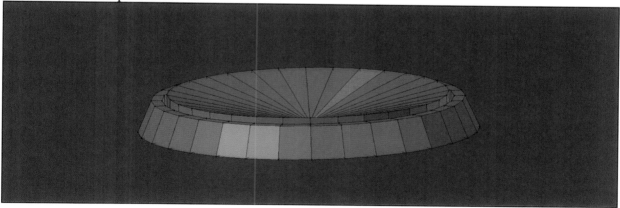

This looks half decent, and all it needs is a Subdivision Surface Modifier and everything will come up roses. So here it is with a Subdivision Surface Modifier added. The depression for the thumb has horrible pinching all over the place. This is caused by the triangles.

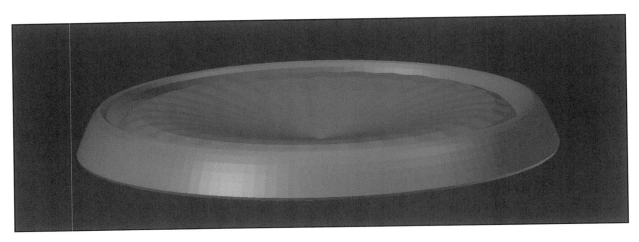

Step 52: The triangles must be tossed out. Select the middle vertex and delete it with X.

Selected

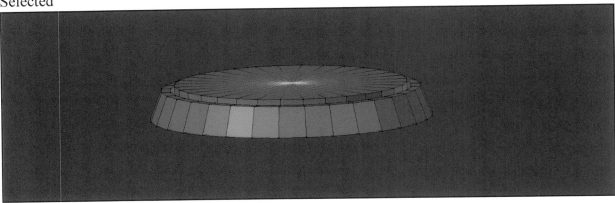

Deleted

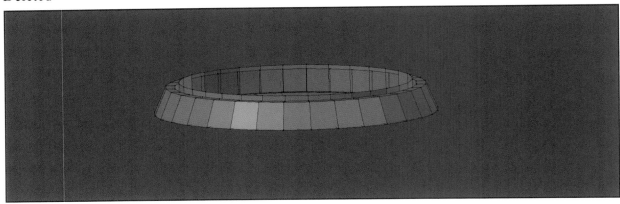

Step 53: The solution from here is as easy as it is elegant. Switch to Edge Select Mode if not already there. Select the top edge with the ALT + Right Click.

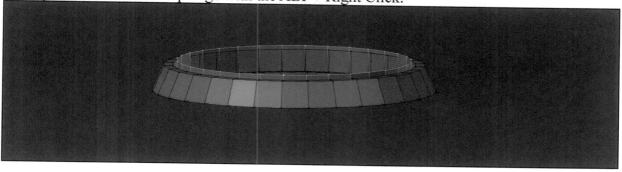

Step 54: Hit 1 on the numpad. The whole idea here is just to repeat this procedure. Hit E to extrude, then immediately finalize the extrusion with a Left Click. Scale in. Keep yours about the same size as mine.

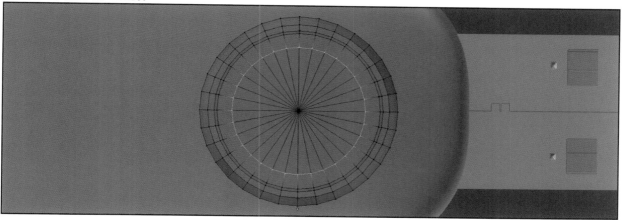

Repeat this procedure about 4 times; each time trying to scale roughly the same amount. Get the scaled extrusion down to a tiny circle. This small circle is the key.

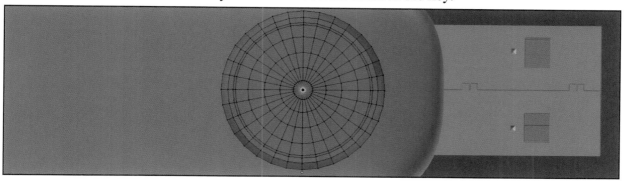

And one last time. Hit E to extrude, then immediately finalize with a left click, and scale in. Then hit W and Merge at Center.

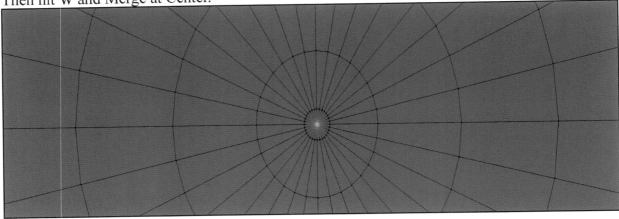

Note: It is very important to discuss what just happened here. The newly scaled extrusions are now quads, which lack the pinching issue of triangles. The only triangles on the top are in the very last extrusion inside what was referred to as the 'tiny circle.' Because the circle is so small, any pinching happening inside of it will hardly be noticed.

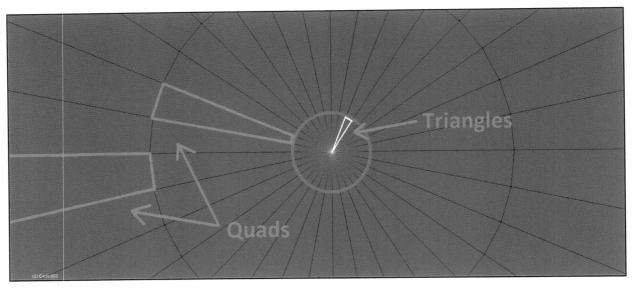

Step 55: Keep the middle vertex selected. Turn on Proportional Editing (to the right of Limit Selection to Visible), and to the right of it, select Sphere. Hit G to grab, then Y to constrain the axis. Scroll the white circle until it covers all the new extrusions, and simply pull the middle vertex down. Proportional Editing does all the hard work. The thumb depression is perfect!

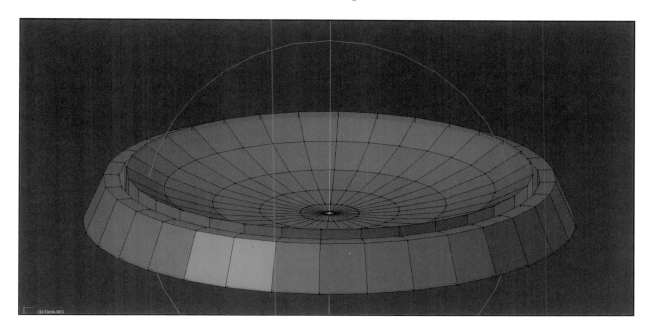

Step 58: Turn Proportional Editing **Off** when finished. People have a bad habit of leaving it on. When unneeded, nothing good ever comes from it. Take a second to check the underside of the thumb joystick. The middle vertex on the bottom should appear pushed down. Grab it with the G key, constrain the axis with Y and place it back flush.

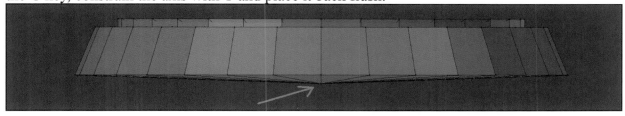

Fixed

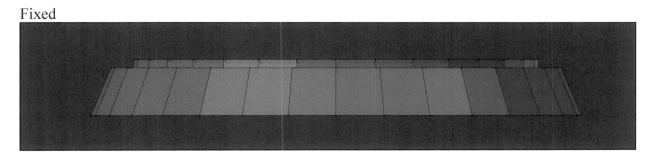

Step 57: Stay in Edit Mode, and add a Subdivision Surface Modifier and set the **View** and **Render** levels to 3. **DO NOT CLICK APPLY!**

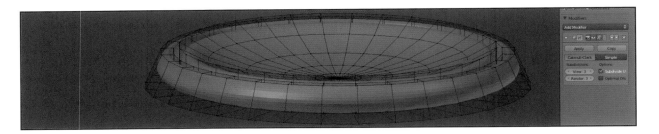

Step **58:** Add a controlling loop with CNTR + R and drag it down to the bottom.

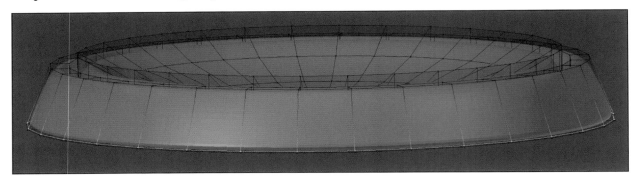

Step **59:** The Subdivision Modifier also smashed down the actual joystick pad and created too much of gap. Select the top edge of the joystick.

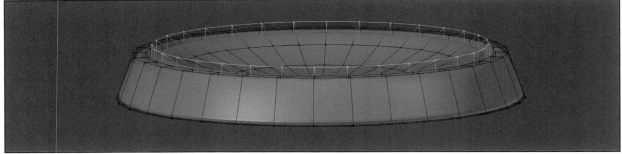

Grab (G key) and pull up on the Y axis. Left click when done.

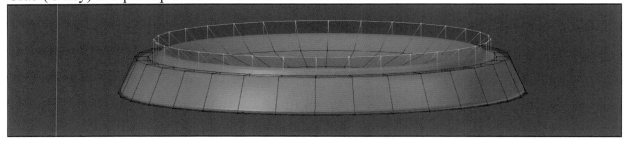

Then hit S and scale it out ever so slightly.

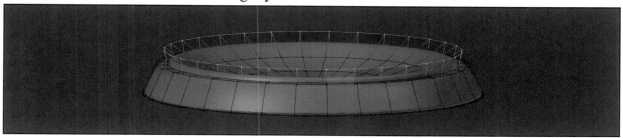

Tab into Edit Mode and check how it looks.

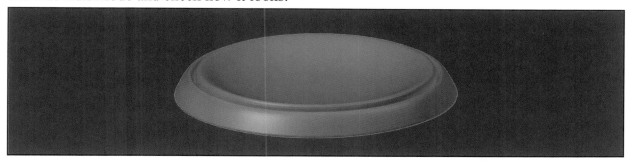

Note: Your mesh may look slightly different and that is fine. Just make sure it looks OK for what it is!
Note: Save the file at this point, USB005.

Step 60: Time for the rocker switch that will be positioned on the left hand side. While in Object Mode, Add → Mesh → UV Sphere. Tab into Edit Mode. Hit 3 on the numpad, select (B key) the right hand side of the mesh and delete it with X.

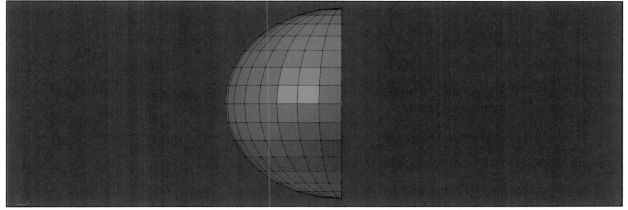

NOTE: Make sure everything is deleted on the right hand side. No hanging chads.

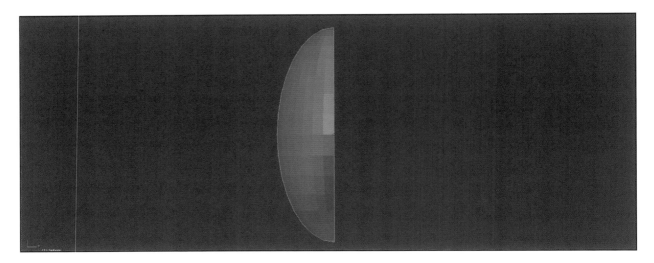

Step 61: Tap A to select the sphere, hit S to scale, and Y to constrain the axis. Then hit .4 on the numpad, then hit return or left click.

Step 62: Hit 1 on the numpad. Select bottom half of the mesh (B key) and delete it.

Note: Make sure the selection starts 1 down from the equator.

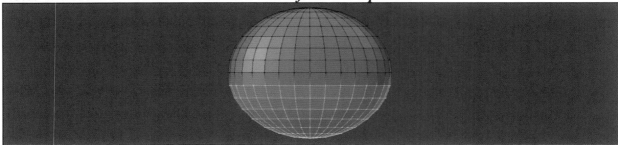

Deleted

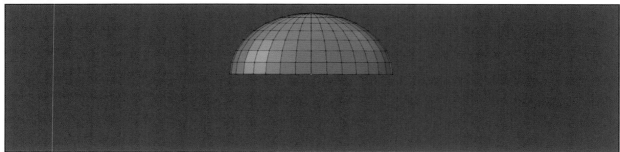

Step 63: Select the very bottom edge.

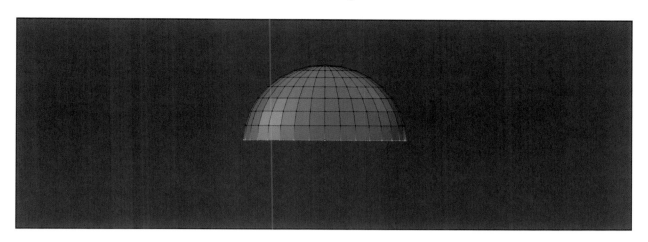

Step 64: Hit E to extrude, Z to constrain the axis, then enter -2.25 on the numpad. Immediately hit return. Make sure the 2.25 value is negative!

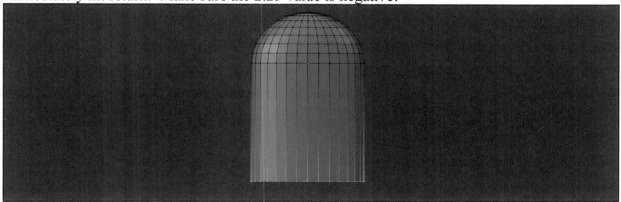

Step 65: Hit S to scale, and enter .45 on the numpad. Immediately hit return.

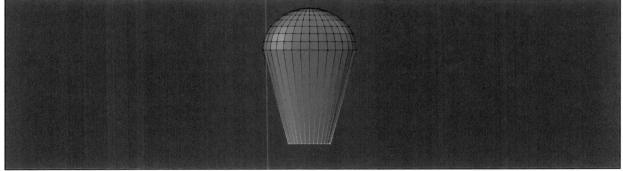

Step 66: Select the entire mesh with the A key. Hit SHFT + D to duplicate it, then R to rotate, and Y to constrain the axis (this will not be viewable). Hit 180 on the numpad and return.

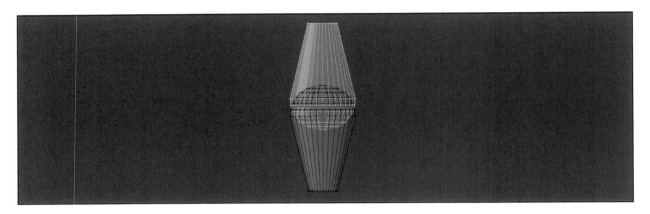

Hit G to grab, then Z and pull it down. Keep a little gab between them. They should not be touching. Tap A when done.

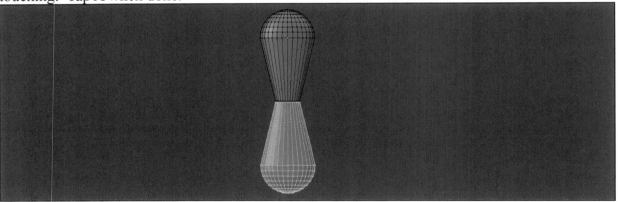

Step 67: The vertices need to be knitted together. Zoom in, select the top and bottom vertices, hit W and Merge at Center.

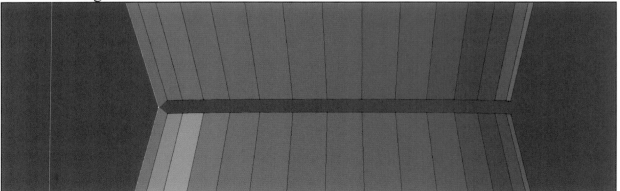

Continue along and do the same for the rest of them.

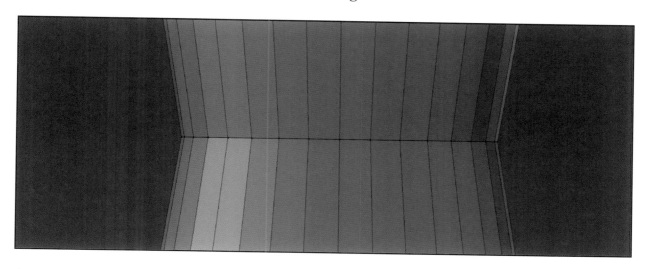

Step 68: And now for the plastic cradle in which the rocker switch will sit. This process is the same as the cradle for the thumb joystick, but it is a little trickier. If an bounding box were to be placed around this rocker switch, it would be a rectangle. Rectangles do not scale evenly, and that makes this tricky. Switch into Edge Select Mode. Hold SHFT + ALT and select the entire outer edge.

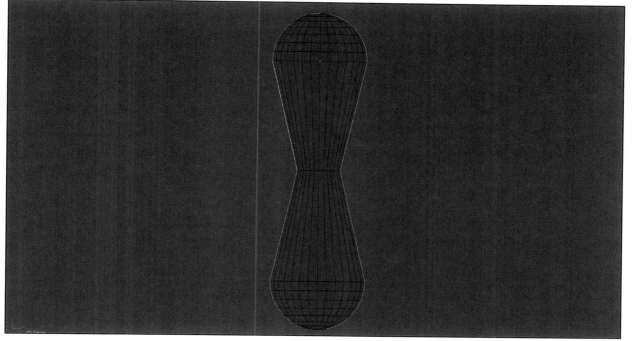

Step 69: Hit E to extrude, -immediately Left Click to finalize, and hit S to scale out just a little.

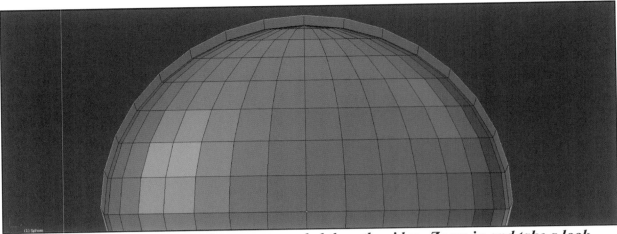

*Note: **Notice how much more the top was scaled than the sides. Zoom in and take a look***

Hit S, then X to constrain the axis. Scale out the sides to even them out with the top.

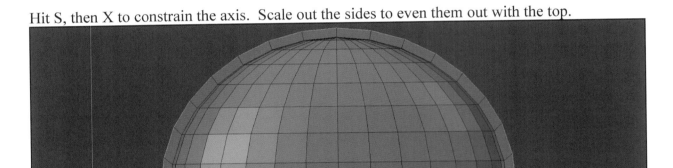

Great, go down to the middle section which was knitted together. Select the left and right vertices (Vertex Select Mode) and hit S to scale them out to be equal to the top.

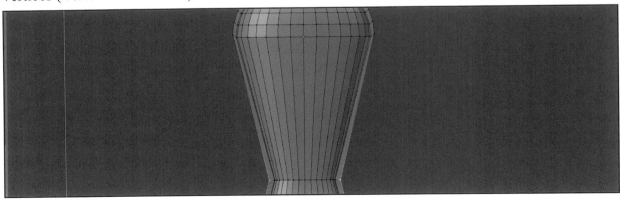

Step 70: Select the entire outer edge with ALT. Hit 3 on the numpad, then E to extrude up 1/4 of the mesh height.

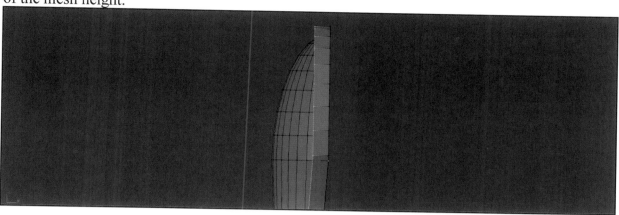

Step 71: Hit 1 on the numpad. Hit E to extrude, and immediately finalize it with a Left Click. Hit S and scale out a bit (this extrusion should almost be 1.5x that of the first).

The same rectangular scaling irregularity is there as before. Hit S to scale, constrain the X axis, and even it out on the sides.

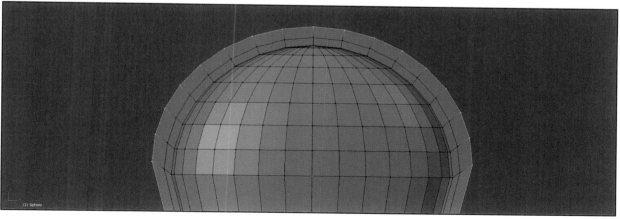

As before, select the very right and left most vertices of the equator and scale them out to match the top.

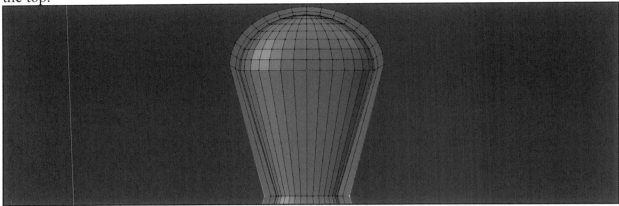

Step 72: Select the entire outer edge with ALT, and hit 3 on the numpad. Hit E and extrude down to the bottom.

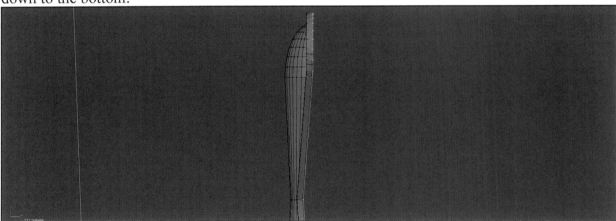

Step 73: And now the slanted angle is made for the exterior rim of the cradle. Hit 1 on the numpad, and scale out.

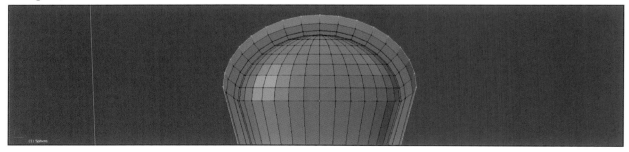

Again, fix the scaling issue. Hit S, then X, and scale to equalize.

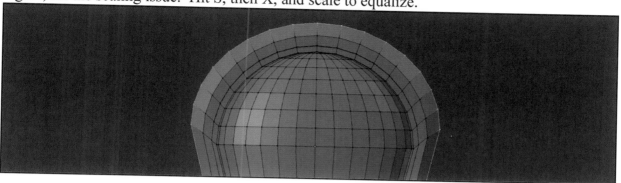

Finally, scale out the right and left most vertices on the equator.

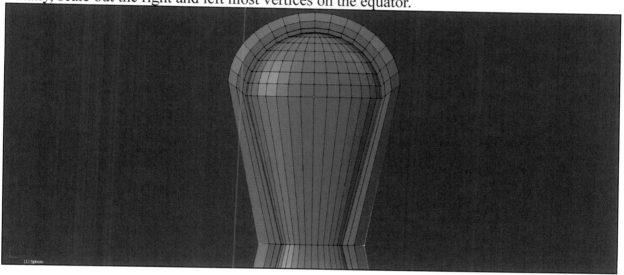

Step 74: With that completed, hit 3 on the numpad. Turn Limit Selection to Visible **Off**. Select the entire equator edge. Hit S to scale, then Y to constrain the axis. Finally, enter .7 on the numpad and hit return.

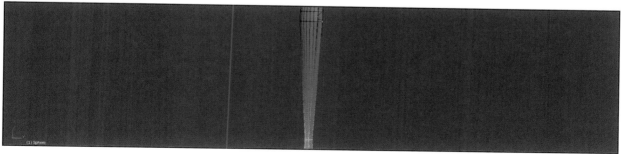

Step 75: Stay in side view, but observe the picture below. There is a curve in the mesh.

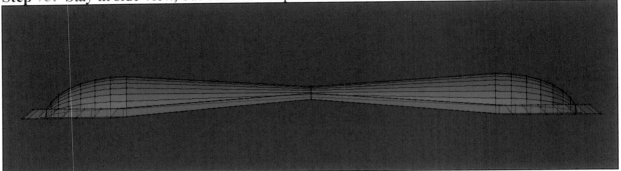

Select the equator region again, and pull it down flat with the rest of the mesh.

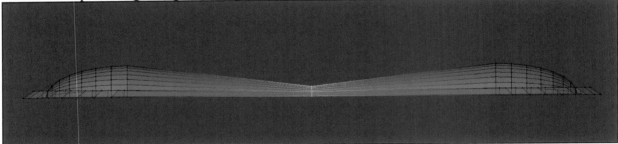

Note: The mesh has been rotated 90 degrees to make this easier to see. Yours will be vertical.

Step 76: While in Edit Mode, add a Subdivision Surface Modifier. Set the **View** and **Render** levels to 3. Tab into Object Mode to see how it looks, **but don't, not under any circumstances, even think about hitting Apply.** However, do hit Smooth Shading in the Tools Panel on the left. Here is a picture.

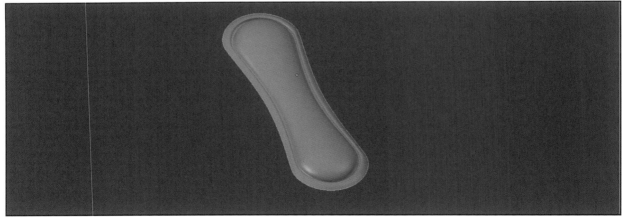

And a side shot.

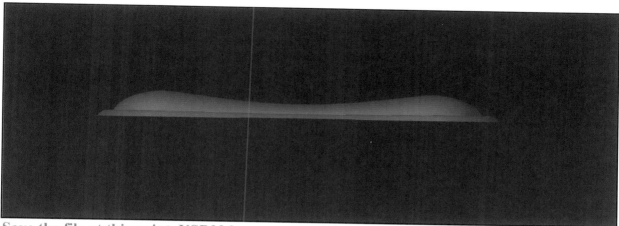

Save the file at this point, USB006.

Step 77: All the modeling is done at this point, go ahead and place both the rocker switch and thumb joystick on the USB drive. They may need to be scaled slightly in one direction or another, and the thumb joystick will have to be slightly rotated to compensate for the downward slope of the USB drive near the head. This is your judgment. If your origins got screwed up, which usually occurs, don't forget about the Origin button in Object Mode.

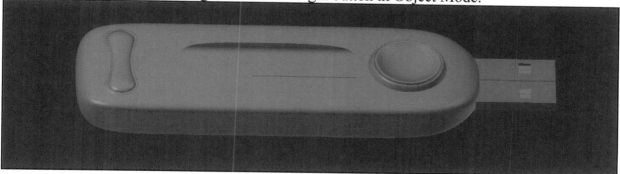

Step 78: And now the materials are to be added. Follow along and use the given materials, and then, if desired, go back and use your own color combinations and settings. In Object Mode, select the entire body of the USB drive, then tab into Edit Mode. Select the Material tab, and click the NEW button. Three settings have to be made.

Under Diffuse, set these values for the color: **Red .01109   Green .008039   Blue .008752**
Under Specular, set the hardness to **24.**
Put a check beside **Subsurface Scattering**, and keep the SSS presets.
Then click Assign (must be in Edit Mode).

Step 79: Tap the A key to deselect the mesh, and switch to Face Select Mode. Select the middle strip of faces as seen in the picture below.

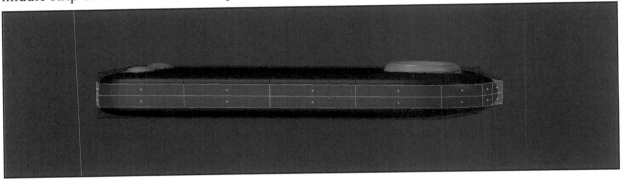

Step 80: To the right of the existing material is a plus sign. Click it.

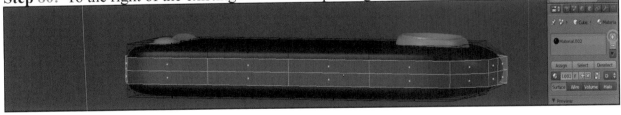

And then click the New Button. Add a new material with the following settings.

Under Diffuse, set these values for the color: **Red .142   Green .001743   Blue .000**
Under Specular, set the hardness to **14**.
Put a check beside Subsurface Scattering, and Select **Apple**.
Under 'Apple', the Scatter color: **Red .380   Green .186   Blue .148**
Click Assign.

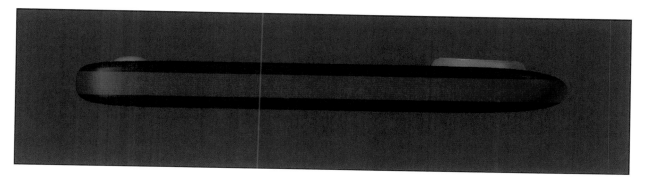

Step 81: Tab into Object Mode. Select the thumb joystick, tab into Edit Mode. Hit the material tab and click the New button. Set the following values.

Under Diffuse, set these values for the color: **Red .142 Green .001743 Blue .000**
Under Specular, set the hardness to **14.**
Put a check beside Subsurface Scattering, and Select **Apple.**
Under 'Apple' -set the Scatter color: **Red .380 Green .186 Blue .148**

Click Assign.

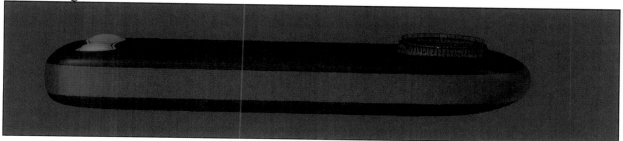

Repeat the same procedure for the rocker switch on the left. The following picture is a completed view after switching back into Object Mode.

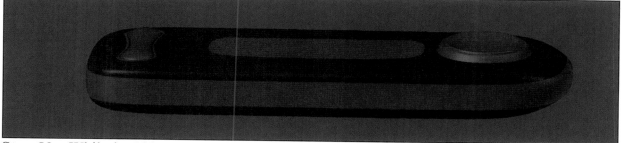

Step 82: While in Object Mode, select the Text and tab back into Edit Mode. Place the text right below where the screen will be.

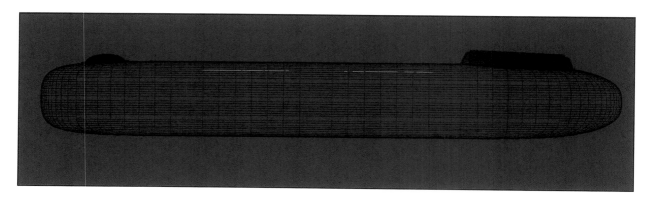

Scale the Text up if needed (a good possibility).

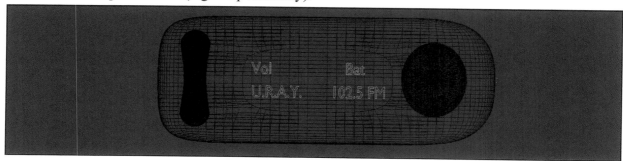

Step 83: Go to the Material Tab, and click the New button. Set the following values.

Under Diffuse, set these values for the color: **Red .258   Green .800   Blue .152**
Under Shading, set the Emit value to: **2.00**

Click Assign

Repeat this procedure for the volume and battery indicator bars (shown completed in Object Mode).

Note: The battery indicators & Text may need to be repositioned (G Key).

Step 84: While in Object Mode, select the screen and tab into Edit Mode. Notice that the screen is not a separate object from the USB body. This is not a problem! Just select the SCREEN ONLY, and add a new material by clicking the 'plus' on the right.

Once the New button appears, click on it and add a New material as usual. Use the following settings:

Under Diffuse, set these values: **Red .08525 Green .177 Blue .800**
Put a check beside Transparency, and set the Alpha value: **.360**

Click Assign, and tab into Edit Mode. The text should be occluded by the screen.

Note: Wireframe Mode comes in very handy for positioning the screen.

Step 85: Tab into Object Mode, and select the USB connector. Tab back into Edit mode. Select the Material tab and apply the following settings.

Under Diffuse, set these values for the color: **Red .271   Green .287   Blue .334**
Place a check beside Mirror: **Ref: .237**

A quick render shows the following:

There is a problem here. The USB connector is metallic looking, but does not look realistic due to metallic objects reflecting their surroundings in a very hazy, unfocused sort of way. This render has none of that. Instead of reflecting the surroundings, or a picture, there is an easier way. Add a Texture to the Material (click on Texture tab), and select Marble as the type.

Only two other settings need to be made. Under Influence, the 2nd option under Diffuse (which is not currently labeled) allows for the amount of diffuse color to be set. Put a check beside it, and set it to .500. The texture color should be set to: **Red .394 Blue .401 Green .471**

A quick render shows the smudge effect, which is hard to see.

Step 86: The last step is to select the plastic insert which goes inside the USB connector. The insert was modeled with the copper strips in mind, but these will NOT be shown. Controlling

the lighting to make them render realistically is out of the scope of what beginners should be mucking around with. Instead, simply add a material, make it Black and under Shading, put a check beside Shadeless.

Step 87: As for the overall render up to this point, there is an anomaly present. This may not be present in your renders: Disregard this step if your renders are reasonably equalizing the colors. All of the Red colors (the strip, rocker switch, and thumb joystick) all have the same materials, but the thumb joystick is rendering darker. Having the center strip appearing lighter is fine, but the rocker switch has to be darkened to match the thumb joystick. Click on the rocker switch, go to the Material Tab, and enter these new values:

Diffuse: **Red .082 Blue .001 Green 000**
Subsurface Scattering Color: **Red .354 Blue .172 Green .138**

That evens out the rocker switch to match the thumb joystick.

Step 88: Time to set up the lighting. It is about as easy as it gets. Only two point lights are used. The light settings are left as 'default'. Additionally, go to the World settings and enable Ambient Occlusion (.75) with a check. That is it for lighting. While there, set the background to Black (HorizonZ, Zenith Col).

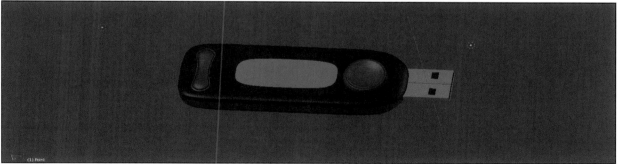

Step 89: For the render settings, set the Resolution to 100%. Put a check beside Anti-Aliasing (this stops the jaggedness) and set it to 16. Do any last minute positioning or scaling. Position the camera and hit F12 to render a shot.

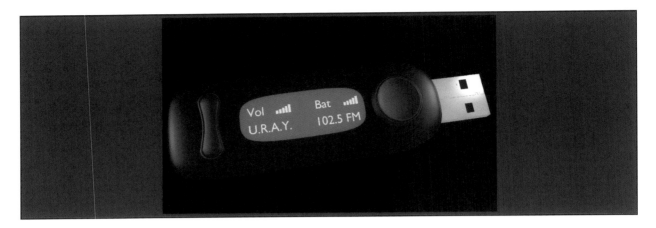

Discussion:

One interesting thing to note with this model was the rendering problem with regard to the thumb joystick rendering darker than the rest of the model. As to why this was happening is a mystery. It could have been caused by a bug in Blender, a memory leak, a memory issue not related to Blender and so forth. Problems such as this occur more often than people like to admit. In some cases, doing a repeated experimentation to isolate the problem is called for, but at other times, a workaround should be sought. When such anomalies occur, gauge your allotted time, and make a decision as to which should be undertaken.

This model is far from perfect at this point. A lot more can be done to make it more realistic. Take some time and experiment with different settings and better color combinations. Save the file first.

Chapter 17: Introducing B-Mesh

Newer versions of Blender will incorporate B-Mesh, which is the new core modeling system. Up to this point, all faces must have either been constructed from triangles or quads. B-mesh allows for n-gons, which is anything other than a tri or a quad. This essentially means that a face can have more than than 3 or 4 sides, and this number, which is initially unknown, is designated by n. Essentially, B-Mesh will allow a face to look as such.

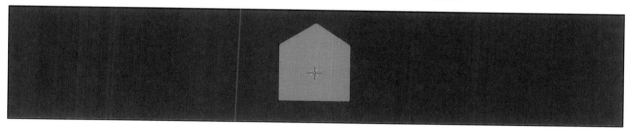

In older version of Blender, this mesh with 5 sides would have had to been constructed from 3 triangles, which Blender automatically creates when subdividing.

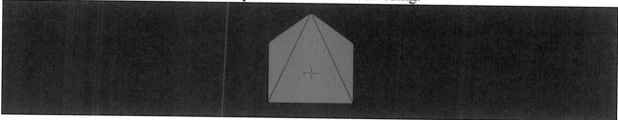

B-Mesh does not anchor vertices (add triangles) when subdividing.

In the older system, the familiar triangles would be added, as such.

To further understand the new B-mesh system, let's take a real world example: The Lanyard hole in the previous flashlight tutorial. With B-mesh, making the hole would be as follows:

Extrude, and then immediately scale in.

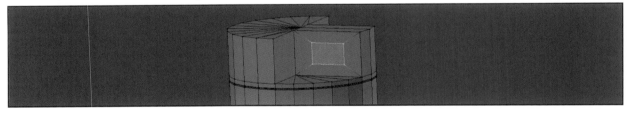

Hit W and subdivide with the new B-Mesh system.

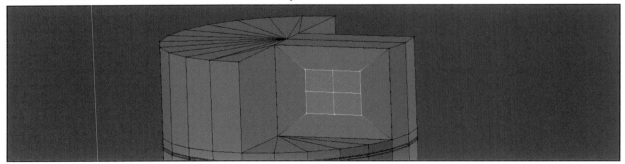

Notice the floating (non-anchored vertices) after the subdivision with B-mesh.

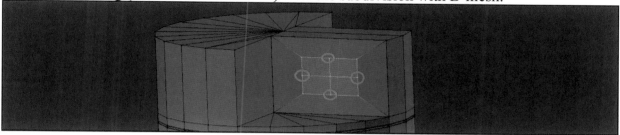

With the old system, the new vertices would be anchored via triangles, and would look as such:

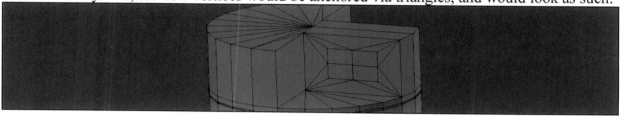

So what is the deal?

The new B-mesh system works just fine, however, it will not work in video games, which require all faces to be triangles or quads (generally preferable as they don't cause pinching issues). It also **can't** be used for final renders using the Subdivision Surface Modifiers.

The following shows a UV sphere with a large n-gon.

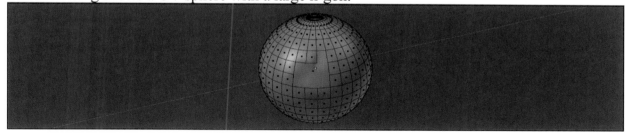

And rendered with a Subdivision Surface modifier applied. Obviously, a problem occurred!

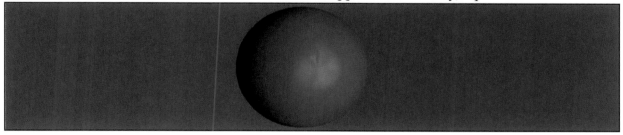

3D Modeling

When doing final renders or games, the n-gons must be manually transformed into triangles or quads.

As shown below, the floating vertex manually formed into a quad.

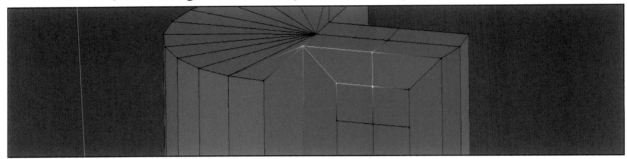

As shown below, the floating vertices manually formed into triangles.

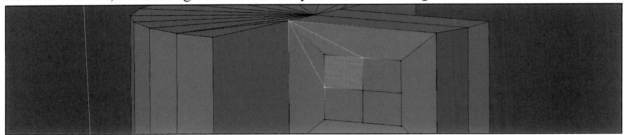

B-mesh was designed out of the box to work with the knife tool. This tool (at the time of this writing) is currently being revamped, and no specifics will be given. However, to get a general idea, B-mesh will allow for shapes to be drawn via the knife tool (k, then followed by left clicking to play connect the dots.)

The following is a simulated example for demo purposes.

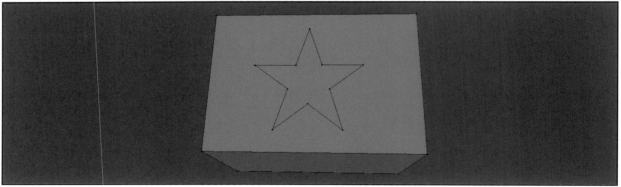

Then extruded

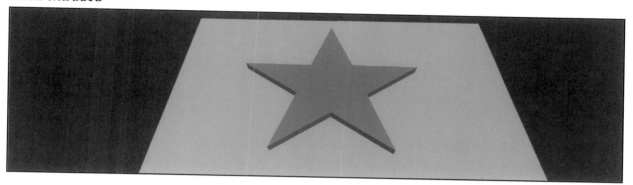

Additionally, B-mesh allows for vertices to be dissolved (with the X key), which is different from deleting them. 'Dissolving' simply removes the vertex, but leaves the face. Take this example, with the center vertex selected.

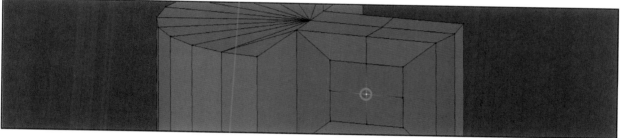

Then hit X, and select **Dissolve**.

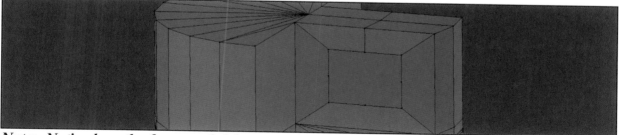

Note: Notice how the face was left intact. This stops holes from being punched in the mesh.

Dissolve can also be used to merge faces into an n-gon. Take this example with selected faces.

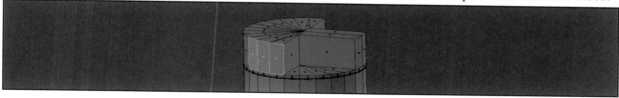

Then hit X, and select **Dissolve**.

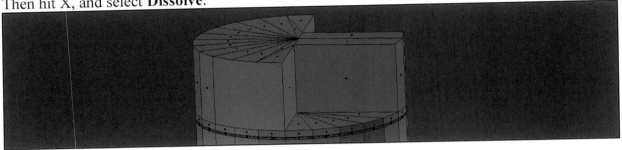

Conclusion:

This served as a very short introduction to B-mesh. There are a few items which were omitted, such as **Collapse** (X), **Limited Dissolve** (W key), B-mesh with the **Boolean Modifier** and so forth; as these items are of limited value, time will was not allotted for them.

Much banter has resulted from B-mesh being integrated as Blender's core modeling system. Some modelers are deeply opposed to it, while others are pleased. It does at certain times increase modeling speed, and this is especially true for those not wanting triangles being formed from subdivisions (i.e., preferring quads); it saves a few steps. In the end, dealing with B-mesh is no great concern, even for those determining it to be undesirable. However, n-gons have the possibility of being terribly confusing for newcomers. It should be very clear as this point as to why this book was taught using a **non**-B-mesh build.

The newest version of Blender has B-mesh incorporated with it. Download and install the newest version at: www.blender.org

----

About your Author:

Justin Hay is a computer programmer, specializing in Java, C++, Python, -with strong involvements in algorithms, artificial intelligence, game design, and modeling. He currently resides in the Greater Pittsburgh Area.